4250

ERRATA:

Captions on page 31 should be on page 34.
page 34 on page 35 and page 35 on page 31.

Richard Lindner

Richard Lindner
Hilton Kramer

A Paul Bianchini Book
New York Graphic Society
Boston

A Paul Bianchini Book
Copyright © 1975 by Editions des Massons, S.A.
All rights reserved.
No part of this book may be reproduced without the written permission of the publisher except for review purposes.
First published in Switzerland in 1975 by Editions des Massons, S.A., 17, Chemin des Fleurettes, Lausanne.
First published in the United States by New York Graphic Society Ltd., Boston, Massachusetts.
Library of Congress Catalogue Card Number 74-78458. Standard Book Number 0-8212-0513-7.
Manufactured in Switzerland by Imprimeries Réunies S.A.

Table of Contents

Acknowledgments

Our special thanks go to Denise and Richard Lindner, for they were enormously generous and patient with all our requests throughout the preparation of this book. We are further grateful for assistance to Julian Aberbach, Claude Bernard, Lee Eastman, Arne Ekstrom, Wolfgang Fischer, Alfried Holle, Jacques Kaplan, Jean-Hubert Martin, Mr. and Mrs. Max Palevsky, Spencer A. Samuels, Katharina Schmidt, Sasha Schneider, Nancy Schwartz, Samuel Shore.

Text by Hilton Kramer

Photo Werner Hannapel, Paris 1974

Richard Lindner

had his first one-man show in New York at the Betty Parsons Gallery in 1954. He was then fifty-three years old, and had been living in New York since 1941. His first great success, however, occurred nearly a decade later—in 1963, when his paintings were included in one of the periodic exhibitions of "Americans" at the Museum of Modern Art. This show coincided with the first wave of enthusiasm for Pop art, and because of the superficial resemblance Lindner's work bore to certain aspects of Pop—its glossy color, its slick surface, and its use of the commercial iconography of big-city street life—there was an understandable tendency to regard him as a Pop artist. Lindner very much admired certain Pop artists, moreover, especially Warhol and Oldenburg, and it was perhaps inevitable that the huge attention lavished on Pop art in the mid-sixties would result in some mistaken notions about the older artist's work, which had been formed on quite different principles and on the basis of a very different experience. Not for the first time did an artist's success have the effect of obscuring the actualities of his art.

Lindner himself was acutely conscious of the differences that separated his work from that of the Pop artists he admired. Interviewed by Dean Swanson in 1969, he spoke of "that European touch of sophistication which, thank God, these Pop people didn't have. I envy them for that." It is indeed a European consciousness of a particular kind that informs his work even where its imagery is so evidently drawn from American life. If, perhaps, his *Portrait of Marcel Proust*, painted in 1950, had been better known at the time, and more deeply pondered, we might have had a clearer account of the complexities harbored in his highly enigmatic art. For there is in Lindner's painting a Proustian reservoir of memory and association, of private symbols and recaptured time, that is quite unlike anything to be found in the work of the Pop artists. The recurrent images and recurrent scenarios that constitute the "secret" of his art draw from this reservoir their essential poetry—the poetry of an exile and an outsider who found in New York the costumes and the *mise en scène* and requisite momentum for implementing the fantasies born of an earlier existence.

Lindner belongs to that lost generation of European artists and intellectuals who were nurtured on the comforts and high culture and cozy repressions of the old bourgeoisie, and were then brutally uprooted by political events, condemned to begin life anew in an alien culture. He is a German Jew, born in Hamburg in 1901, raised in the venerable city of Nuremberg and educated in the art academies of Munich. Until his abrupt departure for Paris in 1933, the day after Hitler came to power, he was well-known as the art director of a large publishing house in Munich. He remains, quintessentially, an intellectual of the Weimar period—detached, disabused, and ironical, deeply knowledgeable about the ways of the old culture and yet possessed of a piercing curiosity about the *nouveaux frissons* of the new world he was obliged to make his own.

Lindner's art thus inhabits two worlds—the world of New York that is dramatically magnified in the garish color and hard-edge forms that are now the basic constituents of his pictorial style, and the world of dreams that has its sources in the romance of his Nuremberg childhood and the pastimes of his early life in Munich. It is an art of fantasy, at once bizarre and outrageous, in which the postures of the mod metropolis re-enact the strategies of distant memories. No other artist of his time has so boldly addressed himself to the sheer pitch and velocity of contemporary urban life, with its mad, headlong, unappeased appetite for the extremes of existence, yet Lindner's imagery is anything but a realistic account of what impinges on the naked eye. He brings an uncanny and painstaking power of observation to his art, but the scene he depicts derives its peculiar force from the graver and more hilarious hyperbole of his own imagination—an imagination haunted by poetic equations between the past and the present. "More and more I believe in the secret behavior of human beings," he once remarked, and as an artist he is, above all, the chronicler of this "secret life"— of all those unacknowledged fantasies and involuntary daydreams provoked by the social and erotic exacerbations of life lived in the maelstrom of the modern city. There is thus an element of the eager voyeur in Lindner's vision, and a shrewd understanding of the voyeur in us, too, for his art compels the spectator to drop his mask of innocence and act as witness to his own forbidden, libidinous dreams. In Lindner's universe there is neither innocence nor any trace of untouched nature; there is only experience and artifice.

The style he has created for this chronicle of wayward, ungovernable fantasies is both extremely "objective" and brazenly provocative. In its formal commitments, it is cool, impersonal, and monolithic, with everything brought to a high finish. There is nothing of the sketch in it—though the paintings are, in fact, carefully worked out from schematic drawings of virtually every detail—and no suggestion of improvisation or process. There is nothing of the "painterly" here. Lindner's style is closer, in some respects, to the tight geometrical style of certain modes of abstraction than to the looser expressionist or realist styles that have traditionally been used in the depiction of urban life or to the romanticized classicism that the Surrealists brought to their portrayals of an interior dreamscape. He can almost be said to be a kind of constructivist who creates his immaculate structures of heads and torsos, of breasts and buttons and belts and lips and eyes, instead of the familiar inventory of squares and circles and triangles. There is always an extraordinary authority in the way Lindner constructs his pictures—a pictorial architecture that is as solid to the eye as a structure made of steel beams and concrete blocks. The light in these pictures is also akin to the kind of light we find in constructivist art—a light devoid of shading or chiaroscuro, a hard, bright, even light that derives from the artifices of technology and owes nothing to nature.

The very coolness of Lindner's pictorial methods, the professional polish and even slickness of his technique are, however, a foil for the heated erotic atmosphere that pervades his work. The detachment of the worldly artist-observer only serves to make the subject matter itself, dominated by images of oversize goddesses in strange dress and temptresses swollen with an appetite for experience, all the more compelling. These figures are outfitted in—perhaps one should say armed with—in the garments of erotic combat. The recurrent tendency of all of Lindner's parintings has been to seize on the far-out changes that have taken place in contemporary fashion design—changes deliberately intended to incite an open sexual response, an invitation to erotic adventure—and then project them on a mythical scale. The exaggerated garments in which Lindner's dramatis personae appear before us, although derived from the boutique styles that are now seen on the streets of virtually every major city in the West, are no more realistic than those fragments of the urban environment which surround them. They are, indeed, pictorial inventions. They speak the language of myth—and in the realm of myth, the swinging styles of the sixties occupy the same world as the costumes conjured up from a distant, old-world childhood. The corset and the sailor suit join the jump suit and the miniskirt. Campy wigs and wraparound shades and skin-tight panty hose coexist with the old coiffures and riding habits. The very rigor of the form in Lindner's work—its highly impersonal mode of execution—intensifies our response to the imagination that is aflame with these elaborate costumes of the buried inner life.

An art so lavish in visual incident requires a certain adjustment in the way we approach it. There is no use trying to reduce it to some skeletal esthetic scaffolding—it resists and mocks all such critical reductions. Lindner's mind is, in some essential respects, closer to that of a novelist or a film director than to that of a painter, at least a modern painter, for whom the "subject," if it exists at all, is often only a pretext for the perfection of a form that effectively eliminates the need for a subject. A film like *The Blue Angel* is a better guide to the world we encounter in his paintings than the paintings of Mondrian. For Lindner's paintings have a cast of characters, a

"plot" of sorts, an action—usually an arrested or threatened action—that can be discerned. It is this "action" that we respond to, and that the painstaking visual intelligence is designed to serve. In the presence of a Lindner "episode," the spectator often feels a certain apprehension and alarm as well as an odd exhilaration and release. We may recoil or laugh, we may be excited or repelled, but the nature

THE VISITOR, 1953. Watercolor, 26 × 20 in., 50 × 30 cm. Coll. Mrs. Ingeborg Wiener Ten-Haeff, New York

of our response is never simply an esthetic response—our experience of life is deeply involved. Something sinister is suggested, and something hilarious, too—for Lindner's world is a comic world, though the comedy is not a particularly happy one. It is a world of power and pretention,

15

THE MEETING, 1953. Pencil, 12 × 15 in., 31 × 37 cm. Private collection

THE MEETING, 1953. Oil on canvas, 60 × 72 in., 152 × 183 cm. The Museum of Modern Art, New York

sexual power and social pretention and the gestures and costumes they assume for the games that are acted out on the vast stage of the mind.

In Lindner's comic universe, there are plenty of male figures, but no heroes. There are only robust heroines who are anything but benign or accommodating. Women here are the figures of authority, agents of aggression ready to tyrannize over male susceptibilities. In this world, all power emanates from female prowess, but this prowess is itself a comic illusion spawned in the fantasy of male vulnerability. For the males in Lindner's imaginary universe are mainly boys—passive and expectant, poised between innocence and experience, waiting for the great secret that can only be disclosed to them by the female predator or the female redeemer—or else they are men sporting the costumes of virility that boys can only dream of, the costumes of the gangster or the "heavy" that were given their archetypal expression in the cinema of an earlier day. The female figure of power assumes many guises in Lindner's work—whore, nursemaid, earth mother, nymphet, ingenue, *femme fatale*. But whatever mask she wears—and her face is always a mask, seductive but unknowable—she is always charged with a voracious erotic energy. She is always in command, ready to give orders, and there is indeed something military in her bearing. Her every costume exudes power, especially the famous underclothes—the elaborate corsets and cruel garterbelts that are somehow more "naked" than nudity itself (which never appears in Lindner)—which have the look of some fantastic military instrument for securing unconditional erotic surrender. There is, in Lindner's legendary women, an almost horrific, devouring vitality. Their bodies assume grotesque proportions which their ingenious garments can hardly contain, but they are the unmistakable proportions of health and well-being, the outsize proportions of a vital force. If there is an element of menace in this fantasy of female vitality and power, it is the menace of life itself, the fearful biologic crux as it makes itself felt in the boy's passive but alert imagination and then lodges itself

in the deeper recesses of the adult male consciousness forever after.

An art of fantasy, then. An art of erotic projection, expectation, fear, yearning, and—however bizarre—gratification. But Lindner's art is also an art of social comedy. It holds an (albeit distorted) mirror up to the crazy, syncopated surfaces of the urban spectacle. The exaggerations are broad, grotesque, and satirical, and the satire eschews all delicacy. At times it is ferocious. The middle class is, inevitably, a special target for opprobrious ridicule, for the metropolis is the scene of middle-class power and imposture, but the ubiquitous whores and gangsters and young swingers are not spared, either. What are they, after all, but the unacknowledged, illegitimate offspring of the middle class? In Lindner's social comedy, there are no class favorites. The bourgeois women are all treated as whores, and the whores are as smug and imperious as their well-heeled "respectable" counterparts.

The atmosphere of money—of money as power, as the medium of dreams, as the arbiter of sexual authority—is everywhere insinuated in this world, but nowhere explicitly depicted. We are never in any doubt, however, that money is the ultimate pornography. In one aspect of his work, Lindner is indeed the satirist of capitalist sexuality—sex as commodity and negotiable fantasy. The whole of society, we are made to feel, is a vast, expensive brothel. Lindner's art has often been compared to the Brecht-Weill operas, especially *The Threepenny Opera* and *The Rise and Fall of the City of Mahagonny*, and with good reason. The evocation of a total and irreversible corruption is certainly similar. So, too, is the harsh parody of conventional social values. The crook and the pimp preside as masters of ceremony, and the ceremonies deride exalted custom. But Lindner's work also suggests comparison with a more recent work of the theater—Jean Genet's *The Balcony*. Here the "acting out" of outrageous erotic scenarios based on the costumes and rituals of power is raised to a metaphysical principle. The Bishop adorned in glittering cope and miter, the General touring his battlefield, the leper yearning to be cured by the Virgin Mary, are actually customers in a commodious bordello. They do their fetishistic disguises of authority or degradation, according to the dictates of their fantasy, for purely erotic purposes, and these can be fulfilled only by an elaborate drama of impersonation. Yet the disguise claims their identity, and there is no easy separation of appearance and reality. Writing about *The Balcony* in *The Theater of Revolt*, Robert Brustein observed that "Genet ... conceives of life as a perpetual masquerade, and *les honnêtes hommes*, without knowing it, are playing a game of appearances." This is precisely the imperative we see vividly rendered in Lindner's social comedy. Madame Irma's final words to the audience at the close of *The Balcony* would certainly serve as an appropriate message to the public Lindner is addressing: "You must go home now, where everything—you can be quite sure—will be even falser than here..."

The most protracted statement of this mordant vision of the city—and, by implication, all of society as at once a brothel, a carnival of deception, and a "perpetual masquerade," is to be found in the suite of fourteen watercolors, produced in 1969, to which Lindner gave the title of *Fun City*. The title itself was, of course, part of the sardonic folklore of life in New York during the late 1960s, used repeatedly in the press and in conversation to designate the rising incidence of violence and squalor that threatened to swamp the city in a chaos of criminal malignancy. Its origin, however, was "straight"—a politician's boast of better times for a city that prided itself on its pleasures. Lindner gives us a series of unforgettable images of what these "pleasures" actually consist of—a kind of sight-seeing tour of neighborhoods and pastimes that parody the conventional visitors' guide to the city, with its innocent promises of diversion and edification. The title piece establishes an atmosphere of gaudy night life—inflated, luminescent pink breasts, nipples pointing straight up, floating like balloons in a cabaret and flanking the gangster's severed head, its smile an obscene

mask, that presides as master of the revels to follow. Straightaway comes a scene in which a criminal is apprehended—*New York Men*—which is also a rogues' gallery of New York male types: criminal (Mafia?), detective, pimp, stylish swinger. Like the other street scenes that dominate the *Fun City* series, this is an episode in the unsentimental education of a

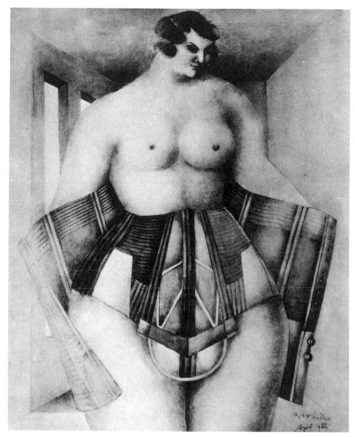

THE CORSET, 1954. Watercolor, 29 × 23 in., 74 × 59 cm. Private collection

tourist out to see the sights and getting a good deal more than he bargained for. (We are never in doubt that the observer is a male.) Everything is conveyed by dramatic juxtaposition and hallucinated exaggeration. The pointed New York City tourist banner, in *On*, with its inset of the Statue of Liberty, becomes a mock phallus joining the naked silhouettes of a man and a woman who are clearly strangers to each other. The doorman, in *Fifth Avenue*, in his elaborate

19

UNTITLED, 1962. Oil on canvas and collage, 9 × 6 in., 22 × 15 cm. Galerie Claude Bernard, Paris

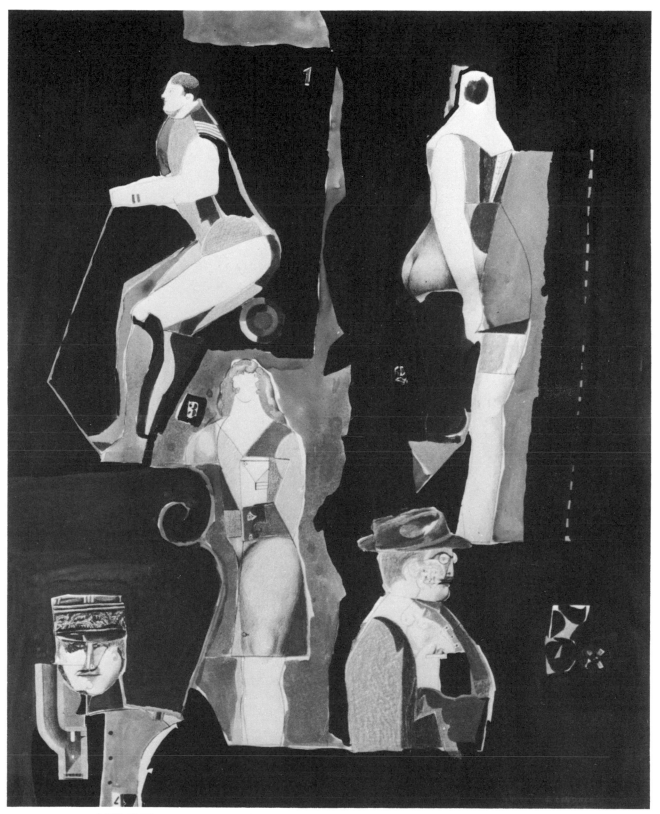

NUMBER 5, 1961. Watercolor, 29 × 23 in., 74 × 59 cm. Coll. Mr. and Mrs. Herman Elkon, New York

uniform of servitude, is a boy-child carrying out the orders of the stout matron commander whose grotesque finery is likewise a uniform—of power and sexual prestige. The young couple in *Shoot*, all buttocks and hair and legs and footgear, exude a menacing strength that is a perfect summary of that atmosphere of corruption we have come to associate with Times Square—once the mecca of the sentimental tourist and now the playground of the hustler and his cohorts—while in *St. Mark's Place* the psychedelic underground is evoked in the hilarious figure of a bearded and beaded hippy prince, the city's new royalty, walking his pet rooster on a leash under the light of the moon. *Fun City* is a landscape of whoredom and liberated appetite in which all the sweet clichés of the old Broadway musicals and Hollywood movies, in which New York was indeed the capital of fun and romance, are inverted with fierce effect. It remains one of the most authentic chronicles of New York in the 1960s any artist has yet attempted—a symbol, if you will, of New York in its "Weimar period."

One is reminded, in all this harsh but comical phantasmagoria of life in New York, of Baudelaire's call, more than a century ago, for the painter who would address himself to the concrete realities of "modern life"—the life of the modern city. In the *Salon of 1845*, Baudelaire wrote:

"No one is cocking his ear to tomorrow's wind; and yet the heroism of *modern life* surrounds and presses upon us. We are quite sufficiently choked by our true feelings for us to be able to recognize them. There is no lack of subjects, nor of colors, to make epics. The painter, the true painter for whom we are looking, will be he who can snatch its epic quality from the life of today and can make us see and understand, with brush or with pencil, how great and poetic we are in our cravats and our patent-leather boots."

We no longer complain, of course, that our artists have failed to seize upon "the life of today" as a compelling subject. This call for a painter of modern life was quickly answered, and in the torrent of images that followed in its wake, the "epic" of contemporary manners and morals, of fashions and fetishes, has been documented to the point of surfeit. From the café scenes of the Impressionists to the drugstore facades of the Photorealists, the objects and textures of immediate experience have been evoked and apotheosized in every generation. Even in an age when many of the most gifted painters have scorned the representational function altogether, we have not lacked for vivid pictorial accounts of the world that "surrounds and presses upon us."

But in the century that has elapsed since Baudelaire invited artists to give us this heroic rendering of all that is "ephemeral, fugitive, contingent upon the occasion" (as he wrote in *The Painter of Modern Life*), the subject itself has undergone a drastic change—a change that is reflected in Lindner's style even more than in his choice of actors or props. The metropolis is no longer an unchartered terrain. Its denizens are familiar types—in art no less than in life. The artificial light of the neon wilderness is now as "natural" to us as the sunset; the cacophonous rhythms and casual violence of the urban throng have long since lost their capacity to startle our sensibilities. Our hearts beat to the tempo of this new speed, and our minds swarm with the imagery of its flickering revelations. The urban environment is now the norm of all existence. The Futurists could still shock the intelligentsia of *la belle époque* with their celebration of machine civilization because the pieties of a pastoral ideal persisted (even where unacknowledged) in the face of the early motor car and the first aeroplane. There remained, too, an entrenched, *passéiste* culture to be challenged and uprooted. There was a frontier to be crossed and conquered.

Such is no longer the case. We live, perforce, in the swim of this accelerated current of fast, perishable sensation—a condition that forces the artistic imagination to alter its basic modalities. In order to secure a plateau of permanent visibility for the symbols of this new, outsize experience, it is necessary to cast

23

PORTRAIT OF MARCEL PROUST, 1950. Oil on canvas, 28 × 24 in., 71 × 61 cm. Coll. Mr. and Mrs. A. H. Ekstrom, New York

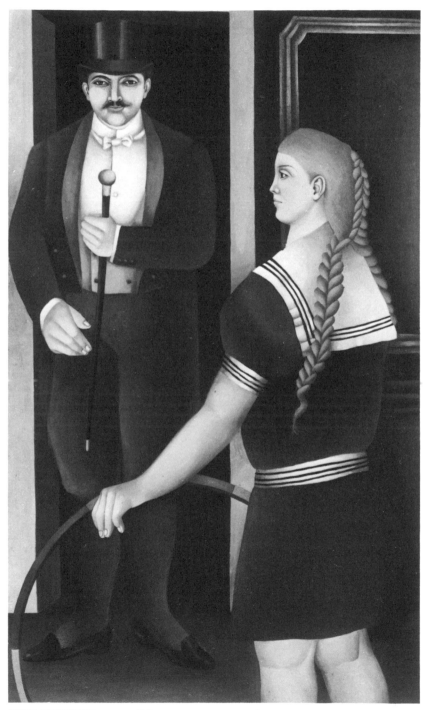

THE VISITOR, 1953. Oil on canvas, 50 × 30 in., 127 × 76 cm.
Coll. Miss Helen Mary Harding, New York

24

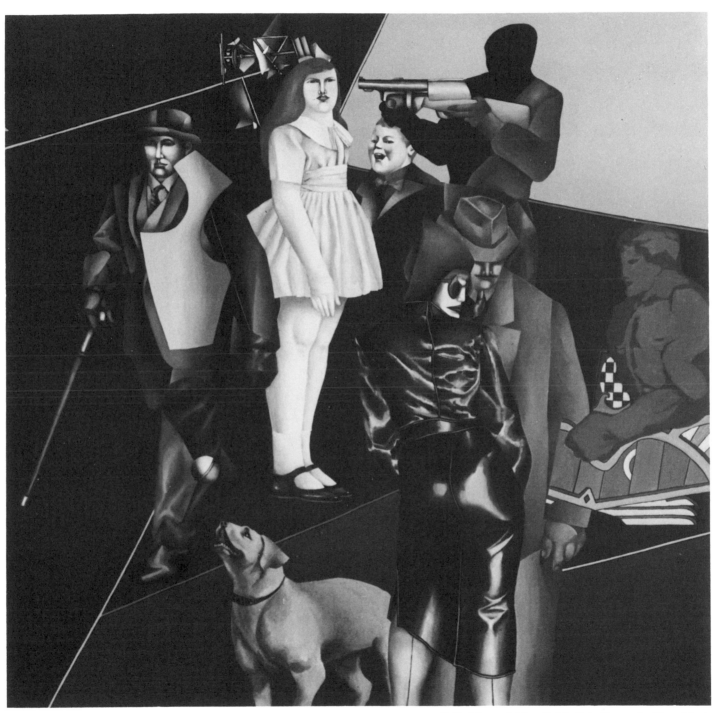

THE STREET, 1963. Oil on canvas, 72 × 72 in., 183 × 183 cm. Coll. Mr. and Mrs. I. M. Pei, Katonah, New York

them on a scale beyond the reach of the very momentum that creates them. Where life threatens to overtake art in sheer marvels of invention and outrage, art is obliged to answer the hyperbole of experience with the greater hyperbole of its own artifice. The dilemma of the heirs of Baudelaire in the third quarter of the twentieth century was given its classic statement in Philip Roth's complaint about "the American reality": "It stupefies, it sickens, it infuriates, and finally it is even a kind of embarrassment to one's own meager imagination. The actuality is continually outdoing our talents, and the culture tosses up figures almost daily that are the envy of any novelist." The vicissitudes of history have turned the bright promise of Baudelaire's "epic" into the rage of Philip Roth's "envy."

This "envy"—the feeling that the artist's task is rendered infinitely more difficult by the tendency of life itself to annex whole territories of the grotesque as its workaday environment—is the fundamental *donnée* of Linder's recent work. It results, among other things, in a more concentrated—perhaps one should say, a more competitive—attack on the present. The *Fun City* series is, in this respect, emblematic of a change that occurred in Lindner's art in the late sixties. The element of Proustian reminiscence is noticeably diminished, and a certain immediacy and swagger are given freer reign. Children—so important in the earlier paintings and drawings—virtually disappear from his dramatis personae in the late sixties and early seventies. The contest—for in Lindner's world there is always a contest of power, always a basic scenario of dependency and authority—shifts more and more explicitly to the confrontations of adult couples. The Lindner couple is a wondrous, frightening phenomenon to behold—a man and a woman effectively and permanently separated from each other by their ineluctable connection. There is no trace of domesticity in their relation, no intimacy even; there is certainly nothing remotely resembling romantic love. There is only an elemental yoke of attraction and a cold-blooded collision of self-enclosed fantasies. There is a terrible bleakness

in these confrontations, and a terrible solitude. Yet the atmosphere in which these couples are held fast, with no hope of escaping their fate, is charged with an intense and consuming sensuality. It is in these quasi-diagrammatic portraits of couples that Lindner has created the most telling of all his acerbic images of the sexual relation in an age of liberated sensuality. And lest we mistake the import of this imagery for an accident of history—only a reflection of a temporary turn in the manners of our time—he underscores its significance as an archetype of the human condition by endowing it with a dimension of timelessness. So, at least, I take to be the meaning of a recent painting like *And Eve* (1971), in the collection of the Musée National d'Art Moderne in Paris, in which the Lindner couple appear as Adam and Eve, re-enacting the legend of the Fall of Man in the mod costumes of the swinging metropolis.

Let us look a little more closely at these paintings of couples. Their design, as I have said, is quasi-diagrammatic. In *And Eve*, as also in *The Couple* (1971), *Partners* (1971), and *Rear Window* (1972), the image is more or less bisected by a sharp vertical or horizontal division. Each figure—each sex—occupies a separate space and a separate color or design environment. Only in the case of Adam and Eve are the figures joined—they look, indeed, as if they were marching together to their doom—but behind them is the inevitable diptych frame, with its spaces allotted for the separation that will occur when their "fall" is completed. (The apple remains intact, but the serpent clearly has the lady in thrall and the outcome is never in doubt.) They are like figures on a chessboard, each immobilized in his or her assigned "square" and each awaiting the move that will result in one or the other's being "taken." The prevailing atmosphere is indeed one of checkmate—an atmosphere of impending defeat. As in chess, too, and in the card games that are evoked in some recent pictures (including *Partners*), the principal action takes place in the mind. In Lindner's sexual scenarios, the mind is the most encompassing of the erogenous zones, the fulcrum of all stimulus and

BOY, 1954. Pencil, 25 × 18 in., 64 × 46 cm. Coll. Mr. and Mrs. Richard L. Selle, Chicago

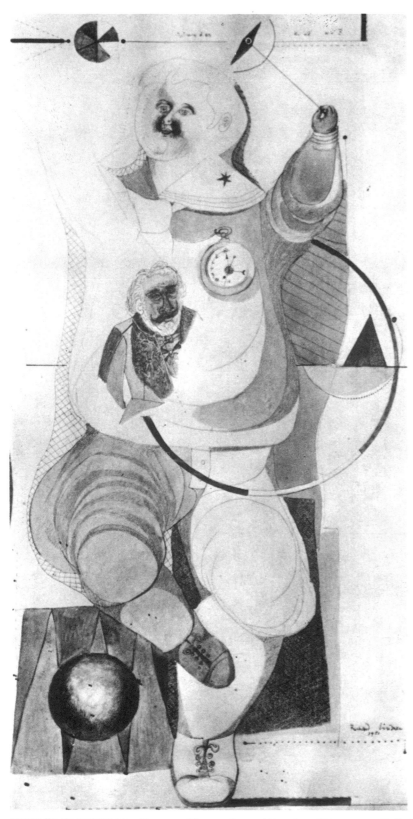

WUNDER KIND No. X, 1951. Watercolor, 26 × 13 in., 66 × 33 cm. Coll. Mrs. Ingeborg Wiener Ten-Haeff, New York

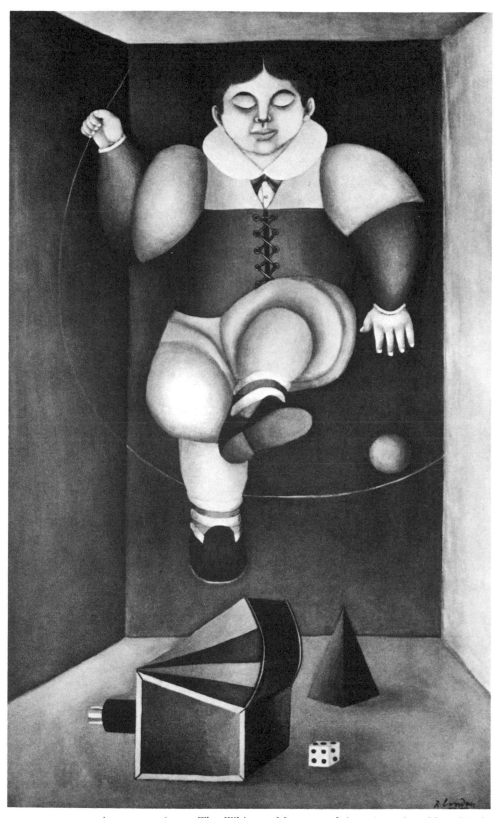

29

THE CHILD'S DREAM, 1952. Oil on canvas, 50 × 30 in., 127 × 76 cm. The Whitney Museum of American Art, New York.
Gift of Mr. and Mrs. Theodore V. Marters

fantasy. This is what gives his paintings of couples their special poignancy and their air of unbreachable solitude, for each of these "partners" is in the position of the woman portrayed in *Solitaire* (1973), playing her game of solitary gratification. The body is depicted as little more than a machine, an anonymous construction of removable parts that can be exchanged in the erotic transaction according to the dictates of the mind. This sense of the mind and the body as separate entities—and the body's adornments as an instrument of the mind's fantasies—is given perfect expression in the terrifying inventions of costume. The structure and proportions of the individual anatomy are mere coefficients of the strategy of costume, which abound in exotic embellishments bearing only a distant relation to the social conventions of ordinary attire. In the depiction of the human body, no less than in the depiction of the environment it occupies, nature is mocked. The size of every member and the shape of every gesture derives from the artifice of appetite, and the seat of all appetite is to be found in the "secrets" of the mind.

Hence the determined rigidity and mechanical precision of the forms in Lindner's paintings—the mannequin construction of his figures and heads and the mask-designed faces. There is an echo in all this of a German artist of the Bauhaus period Lindner much admires—Oskar Schlemmer, whose mechanical ballet figures were similarly constructed to resemble machine-tooled inventions. Schlemmer aspired to an ideal conception of the human figure, a figure that would take its place as the most important element in a transcendent geometrical vision. The human body became, for Schlemmer, a kind of metaphysical integer, and thus no longer subject to the accidents of a psychological resident of the earthly environment. This conception of the human subject is very different, of course, from the one animating Lindner's pictorial universe, yet in one crucial respect both artists are engaged in a similar task—the task of reconstructing a human prototype from the evidence of the mind. Both abjure the easy evidence of social convention as an inferior fiction, and seek instead some fundamental archetype from which to recreate the human image. But whereas Schlemmer found this archetype in the abstractions of romantic metaphysics, Lindner located it in the will to fantasy—in the mind's compulsion to fabricate an imaginary universe out of its encounters with ordinary experience. This difference allows Lindner's art to traffic in the materials of the vulgar world without placing it under the obligation to record them with commonplace fidelity. The only verisimilitude to be observed in this rendering of a prototype that is no less "abstract" than Schlemmer's is that of the mind's inventions. It is in this respect, above all, that Lindner remains an artist in the German tradition—an artist for whom the visible is the outward expression of an interior, "hidden" universe.

Lindner's style is likewise "German" in its basic affinities. Its hard surface eschews all painterly nuance, and thus effectively resists any reading of the "hand" that executes it. It is a style that betrays no imperfections, hesitancies or second thoughts, and thus offers no openings through which we may glimpse the artist's soul. It is a studied style, aggressively "objective," that succeeds in covering its tracks. As is usually the case with the German masters, it is firmly based on the discipline of an expert draftsmanship. The pencil is given unmistakable authority over the brush, and Lindner's is a pencil well schooled in the practices of both the classical draftsman and the commercial illustrator. In his drawing style, the "high" purity and elegance of the one tradition and the "low" caricature and vernacular distortion of the other are easily joined. It follows that color, which is so tremendously important to the emotional effect of Lindner's painting, performs only an ancillary function in determining its forms. These invariably derive from precisely drawn contours and graphic silhouettes, which it is the role of color to supply with appropriately provocative intensities of eye-filling sensation. Lindner's color has grown more and more daring in its taste for glaring densities of the most "artificial" brightness. He is a

GIRL, 1958. Crayon and watercolor, 26 × 15 in., 66 × 38 cm. Coll. Mr. and Mrs. Max Palevsky, Los Angeles

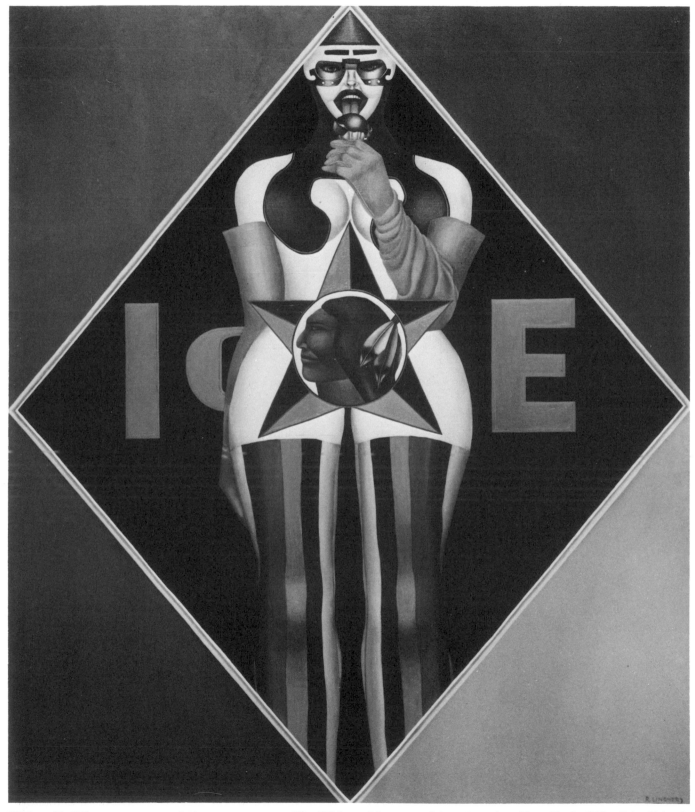

ICE, 1966. Oil on canvas, 70 × 60 in., 178 × 153 cm. The Whitney Museum of American Art, New York. Gift of the Friends of the Whitney Museum of American Art

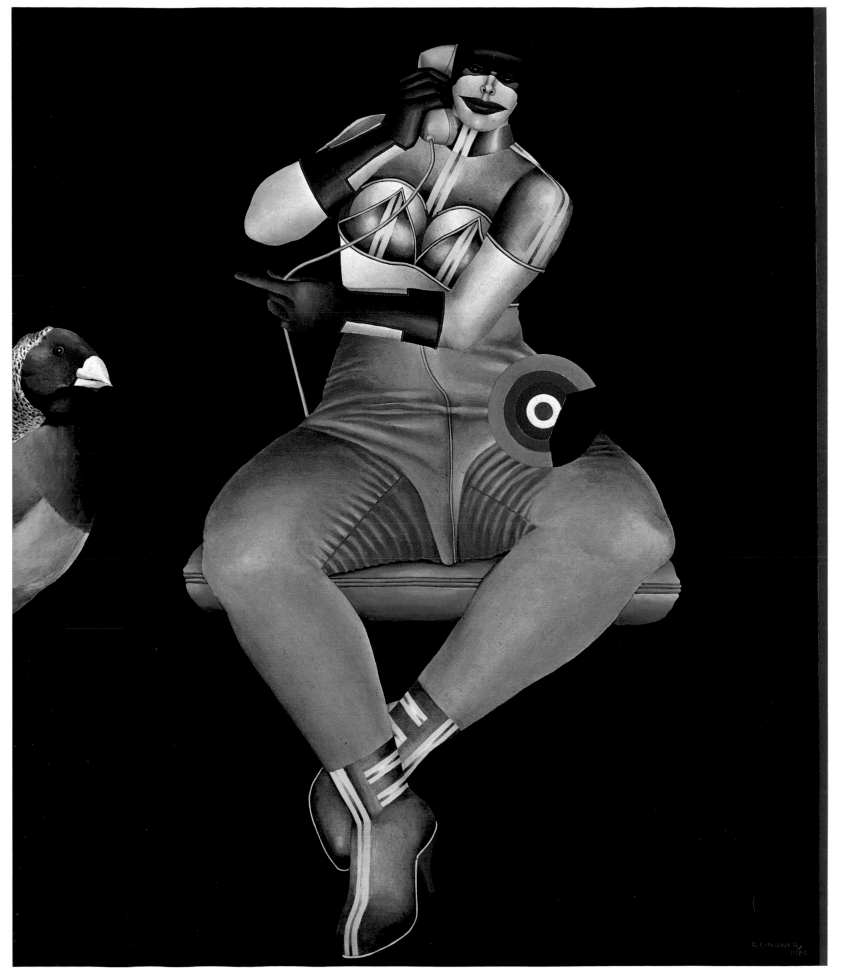

HELLO, 1966. Oil on canvas, 70 × 60 in., 178 × 153 cm. Coll. Harry N. Abrams Family, New York

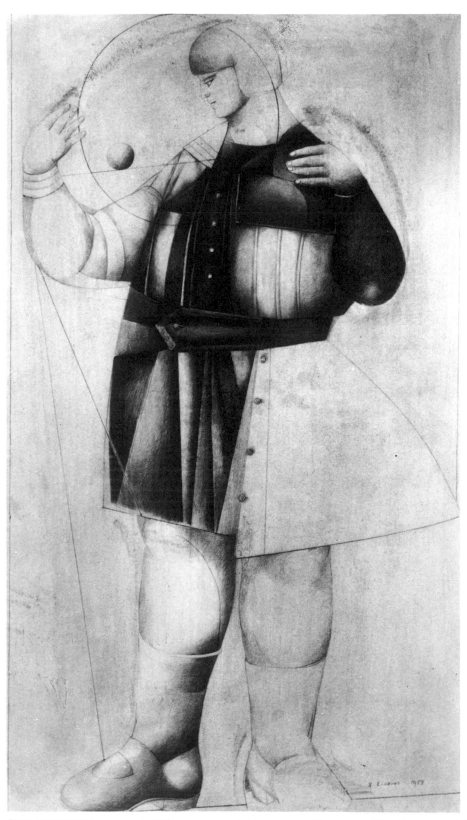

34 STRANGER No. 2, 1958. Oil on canvas, 60 × 40 in., 153 × 102 cm. The Trustees of the Tate Gallery, London

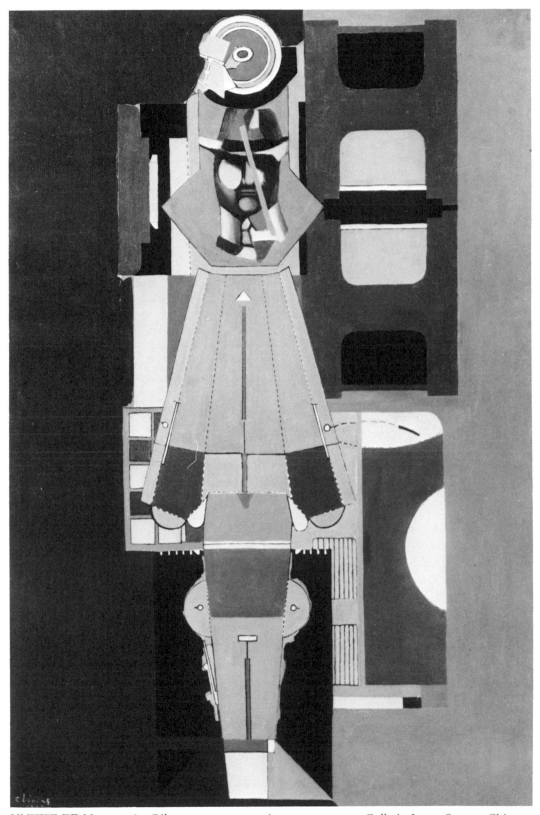

UNTITLED No. 2, 1962. Oil on canvas, 79 × 50 in., 200 × 127 cm. Coll. A. James Speyer, Chicago

master at orchestrating the most flamboyant chromatic choices, and he is both immensely skillful and wonderfully sly at infusing this bold color with a sardonic humor. He is a virtuoso technician, too, in the application of this color, providing each of its discreet units with the exact weight and texture and luminosity his conception calls for. But the conception itself is graphic rather than chromatic. The syntax of Lindner's painting remains a draftsman's syntax. What the artist is concerned to offer us is a dazzling harlequinade, and to this end every figure, every gesture and facial expression, every detail of the décor must be very precisely "illustrated." The space in which this harlequinade is set is a modified Cubist space—the Cubism of Picasso's *Three Musicians* and Léger's *Three Women* redrawn along the lines of the flatter, leaner, hard-edge styles of the sixties. It is an urban, angular space in which the very structure of each component is designed to function as the scenery of a dream. It is a space, moreover, more akin to the space of the screen than to that of the stage, for this harlequinade unfolds as a succession of close-ups, split-screen juxtapositions, and pictorial montage.

Whatever affinities may be divined between Lindner's style and the art of the period in which he has been actively at work in New York—and these affinities extend, as I have suggested, quite as much to the new abstract painting as to the Pop movement—his art seems deliberately to locate itself outside the usual imperatives of art history. From the first major work Lindner produced in America—*The Meeting* (1953), now in the collection of the Museum of Modern Art in New York—he placed his painting at an emphatic distance from what "advanced" opinion regarded as a permissible option. Dore Ashton has correctly characterized this painting as Lindner's "initial declaration of independence"—the painting in which the artist-exile both summed up his experience and stated his artistic interests. There was something more involved here than simply choosing to paint in a representational style in the heyday of abstraction. A fundamental attitude toward the pictorial medium was given unequivocal definition. Whereas the concerns of the New York School were primarily esthetic concerns, Lindner's were primarily existential. It was the nature of his experience he wished to explore in painting, rather than the nature of the medium. While it remained a basic article of faith for the Abstract Expressionists to refuse to traffic in pictorial illusion, Lindner committed his art irrevocably to the illusionist devices of the medium, finding in them the perfect vehicle for exploring the illusionist compulsions of the mind.

The Meeting is the most autobiographical of all Lindner's paintings—a rich Proustian amalgam of private reminiscence and symbolic evocation, at once a family romance and a chronicle of cultural change. The childhood of the artist is represented in the figure of the young boy in a sailor suit, and the artist's new life, in the portraits of his artist friends, Saul Steinberg (seated), Hedda Sterne (upper right), and Evelyn Hofer (lower left). The central action, however, consists of a dramatic confrontation between the old world and the new, in which the figure of the mad King Ludwig of Bavaria, representing Europe in all its gorgeous decadence and esthetic extravagance, is faced by the corsetted temptress—Lindner's archetypal whore of the metropolis—and her promise of a devouring vitality. Thus are the terms drawn up for Lindner's American scenario, and his paintings thereafter become a succession of initiations into new experience, still haunted in its early stages by the child figures that represent innocence and passivity in the face of knowledge and temptation, but, from the sixties onward, dominated by the demonic energies and fantasies of the new world. We move from the private chamber of old memories and associations to the public space of the street, which is the scene of another order of illusion. And what we feel in all this, as Lindner takes possession of his new mythology, is both a tremendous sense of release and liberation and a terrifying mordancy—that encapsulating irony which sooner or later turns the entire human enterprise into a comedy of gratification and a brutal contest of authority. Lindner's comedy is, after all, a comedy of horrors in which primitive instinct traduces all moral delicacy. His stock company of queening whores, hustlers, and gangsters in uncontested positions of power, of men and boys in uniforms and attitudes of dependency and servitude, of animals stripped of their natural force and domesticated into scenarios of service—all this traces a grim drama of social degeneration. The strange gaiety and macabre detachment of Lindner's art are, finally, only a form of stoicism in the face of some primordial disaster restaged in modern dress.

Lindner's work, taken as a whole, is a powerful statement of the dislocations of the modern psyche, and a commentary on modern history. For there is a distinct historical dimension to the air of anxiety and menace that pervades his work. He is not, in any obvious sense, a "political" artist, but there is nonetheless a hidden political substratum to the atmosphere one encounters in this harlequinade of the modern city. The contest of power has been transferred to the realm of erotic revery, yet the sense of harsh conflict and the will to dominance—the awful

sense of vulnerability on the part of the victim, the general aura of a merciless universe—cannot entirely be accounted for in sexual terms. The "action" one discerns in Lindner's art is somehow larger and more malevolent than the protagonist's erotic psychodrama. The refugee forced into alien and unfriendly circumstance by the vicissitudes of history is subsumed in the persona of the passive boy-child awakened to the threat of his biological fate. The political hoodlums of the old world reappear in the costumes of the new liberation. There is an almost Darwinian identification of political power and sexual dominance in Lindner's complex vision of life. The innocent are condemned to be eternal victims, the victims eternal collaborators in their own undoing. The echoes of Weimar and the Hitler era are unmistakable, yet it is no evocation of distant history that Lindner's art discloses. Its commanding irony is to be found in the fact that the scenarios of the past prove to be a perfect index to the emotions of the present.

Hilton Kramer

Plates

All drawings reproduced in this section were made on tracing paper. None is larger than twelve inches in either direction. The following abbreviations are used in the captions: c/p/c/p for crayon and pencil with collage on paper, o/c for oil on canvas, w/c/p for watercolor and collage on paper, w/p for watercolor on paper, w/p/p for watercolor and pencil on paper and Priv. Coll. for private collection.

NEW YORK MEN, 1968
w/p, 24 × 20 in., 61 × 51 cm.
Galerie Claude Bernard, Paris

41

43

ON, 1968
w/p, 24 × 20 in., 61 × 51 cm.

Spencer A. Samuels & Co., New York

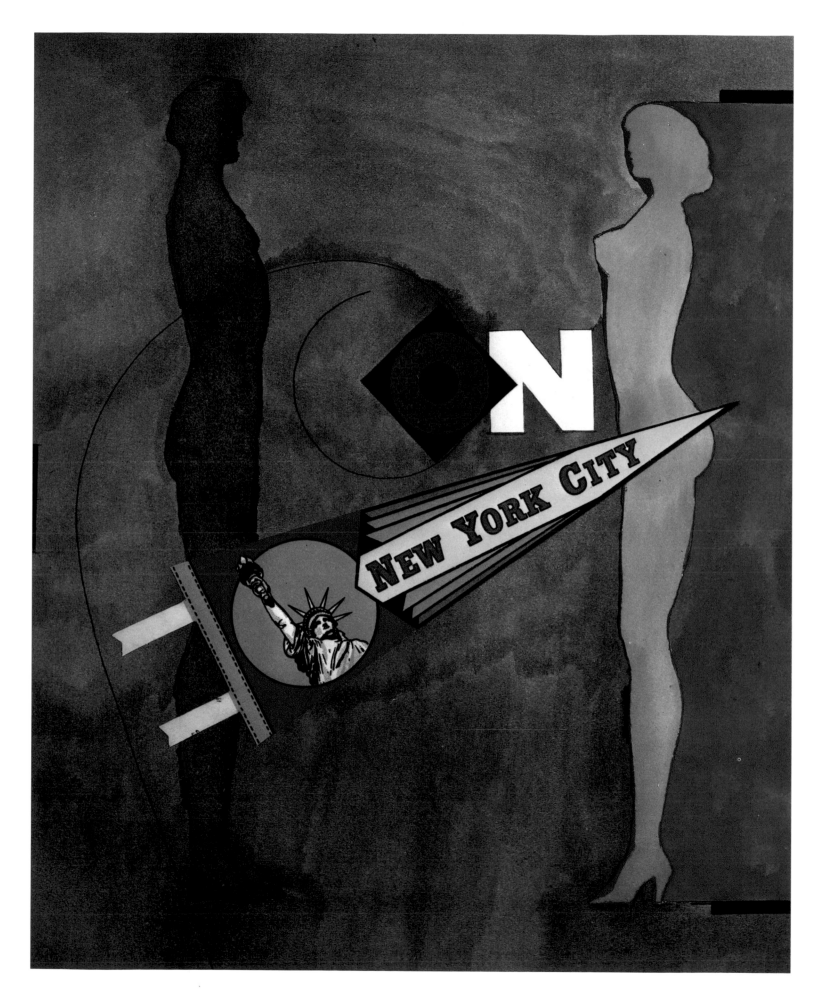

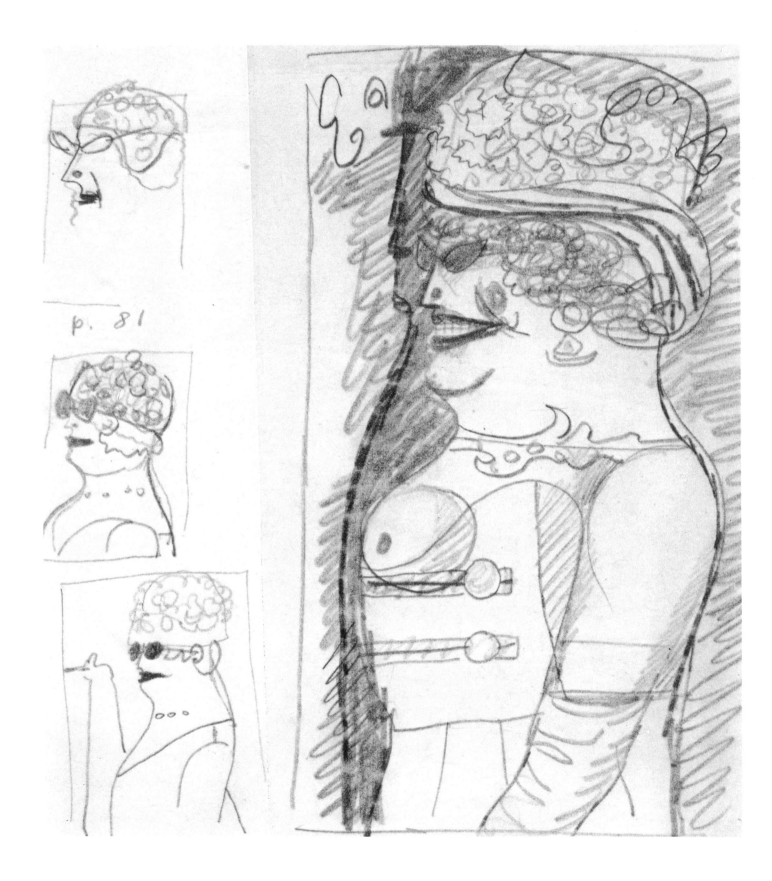

p. 81

46

FIFTH AVENUE, 1968
w/p, 24 × 20 in., 61 × 51 cm.
Coll. William Zierler, New York

49

FIRST AVENUE, 1968
w/p, 24 × 20 in., 61 × 51 cm.
Galerie Beyeler, Basel

24 HOUR SELF-SERVICE, 1968
w/p, 24 × 20 in., 61 × 50 cm.
Coll. Playboy Enterprises, New York

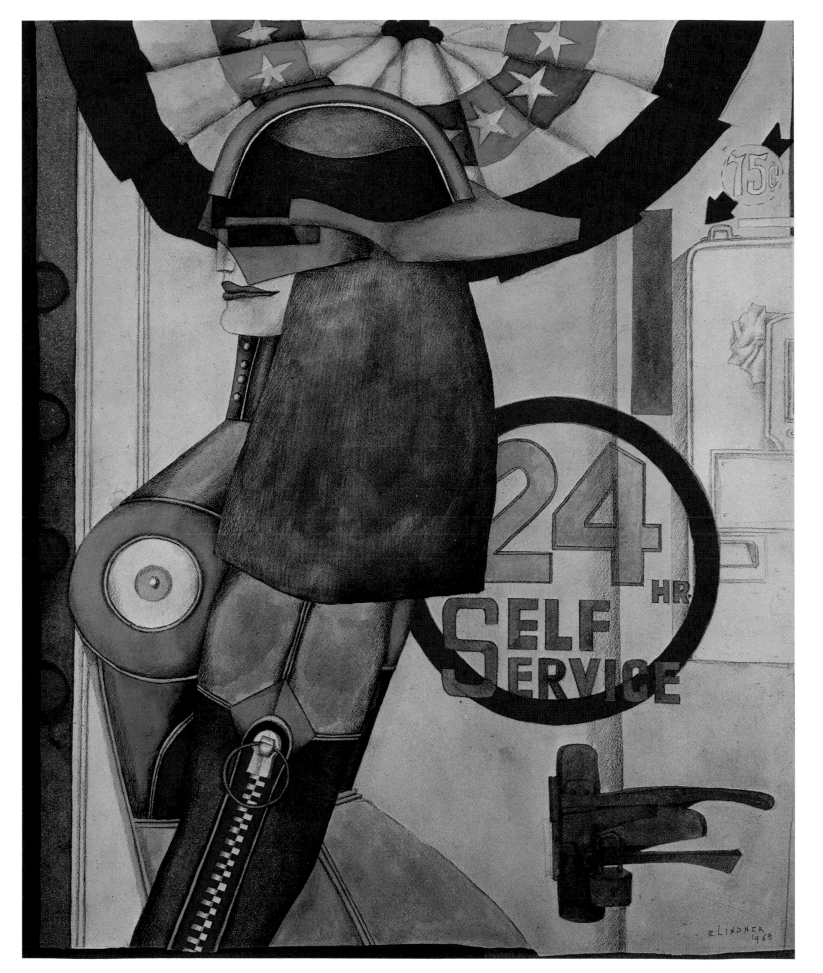

ARTURO UI, 1968
w/p, 30 × 20 in., 76 × 51 cm.
Coll. Rhode Island School
of Design, Providence

56

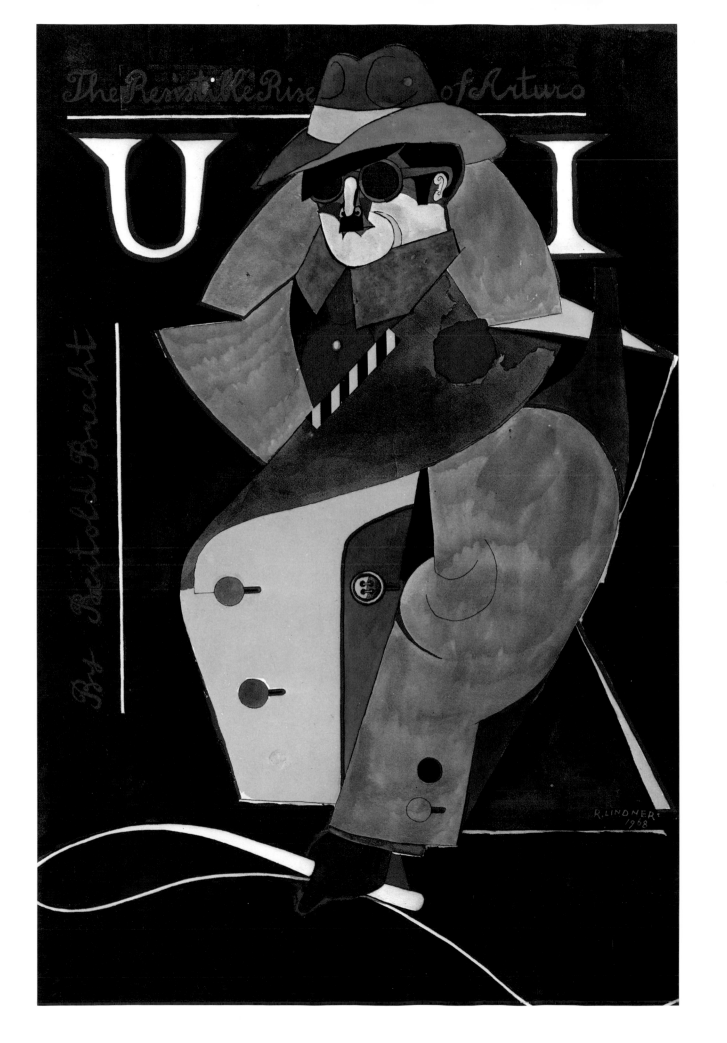

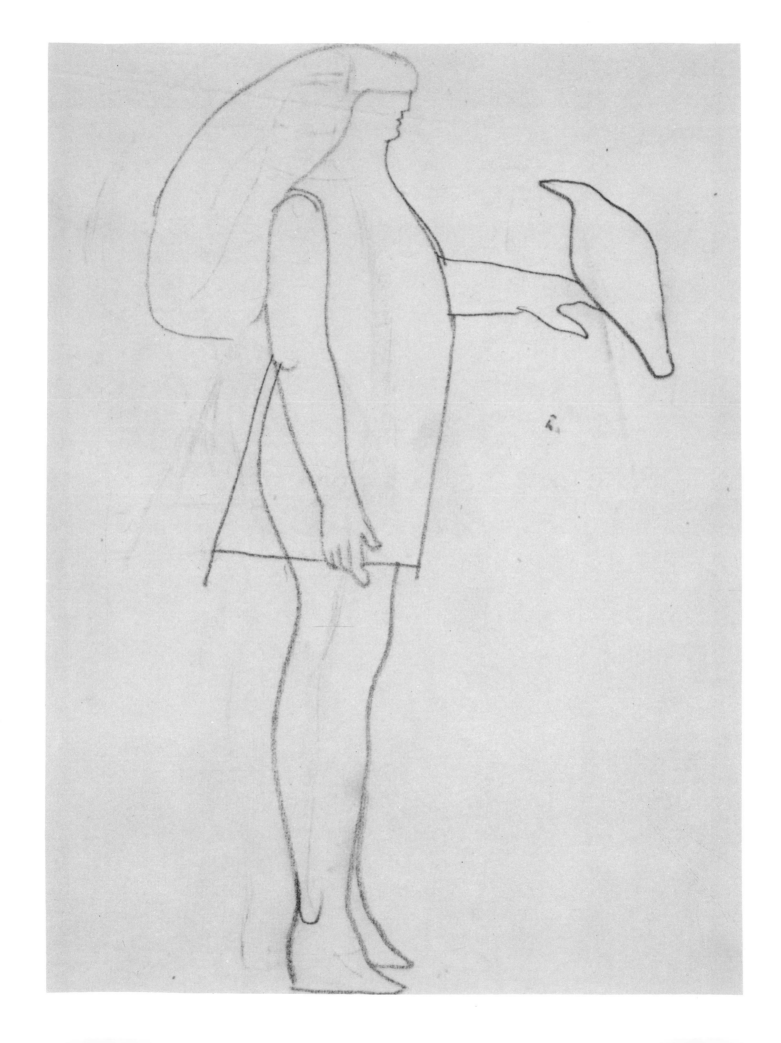

58

TO SASHA, 1968
w/p, 15 × 11 in., 39 × 28 cm.
Coll. Alexander Schneider,
New York

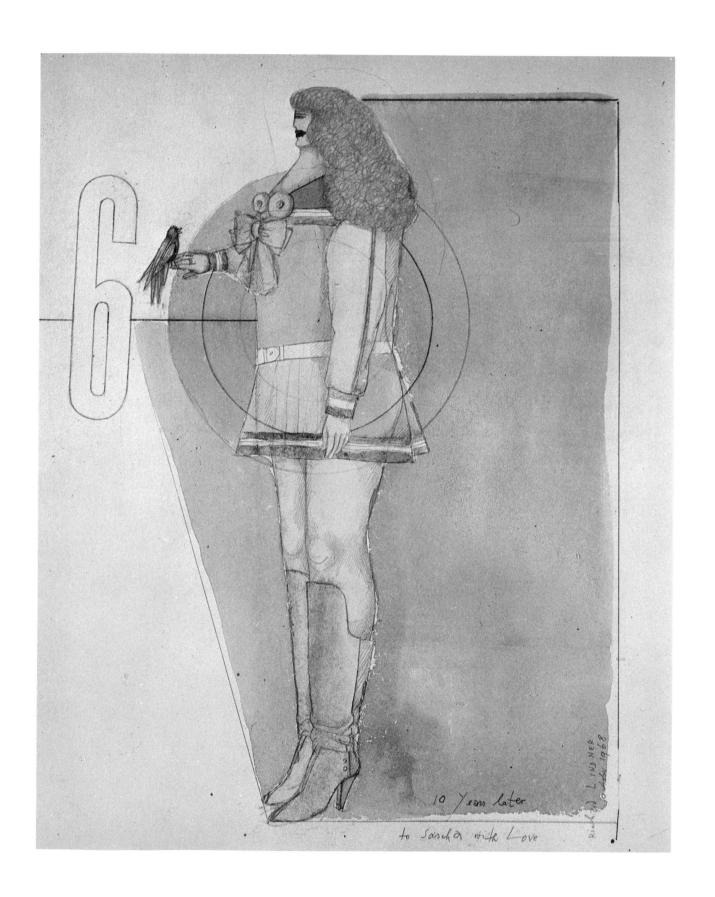

61

POET (Portrait of Ginzburg), 1968/69
w/p, 24 × 20 in., 61 × 50 cm.
Knoedler Gallery, Inc., New York

OUT OF TOWNERS, 1968
w/p, 24 × 21 in., 61 × 50 cm.
Priv. Coll.

FUN CITY, 1969, w/p, 27 × 40 in., 69 × 102 cm. Coll. Hal Reed, New York

SHOOT I, 1969
w/p, 41 × 29 in., 104 × 74 cm.
Galerie Claude Bernard, Paris

SHOOT II, 1969
w/p, 41 × 29 in., 104 × 74 cm.
Galerie Claude Bernard, Paris

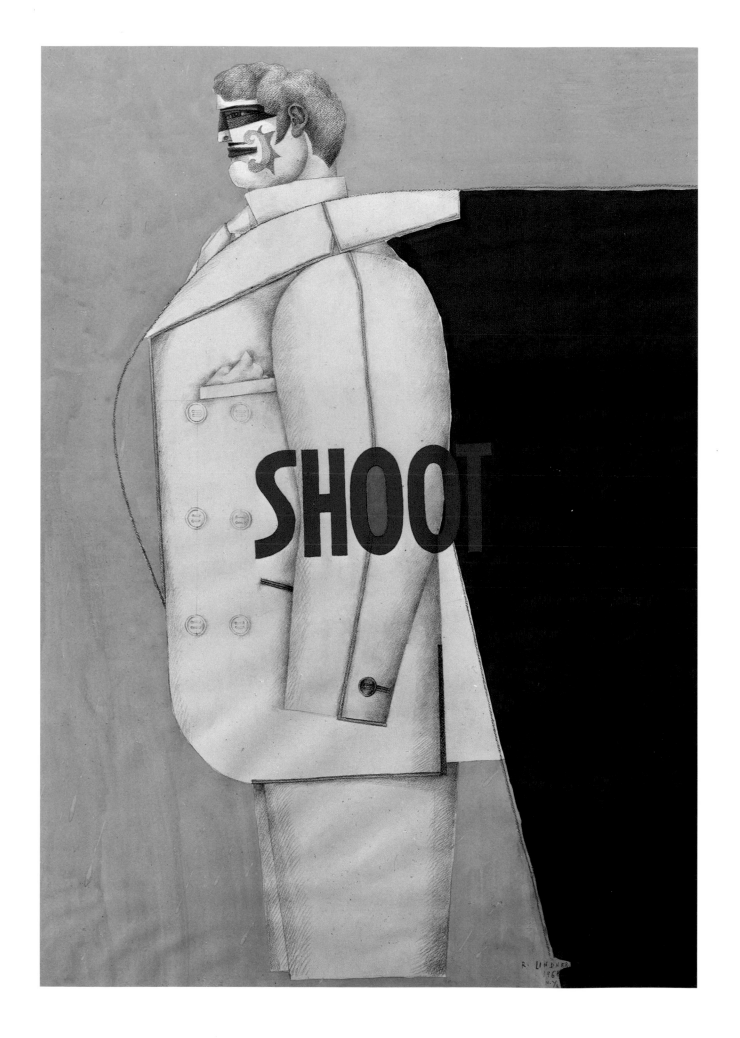

SHOOT III, 1969
w/p, 41 × 29 in., 104 × 74 cm.
Galerie Claude Bernard, Paris

77

GIRL WITH HOOP, 1969, w/p, 24 × 20 in., 61 × 51 cm. Priv. Coll.

UPTOWN, ca. 1969
w/p, 24 × 20 in., 61 × 51 cm.
Coll. Sam Shore, New York

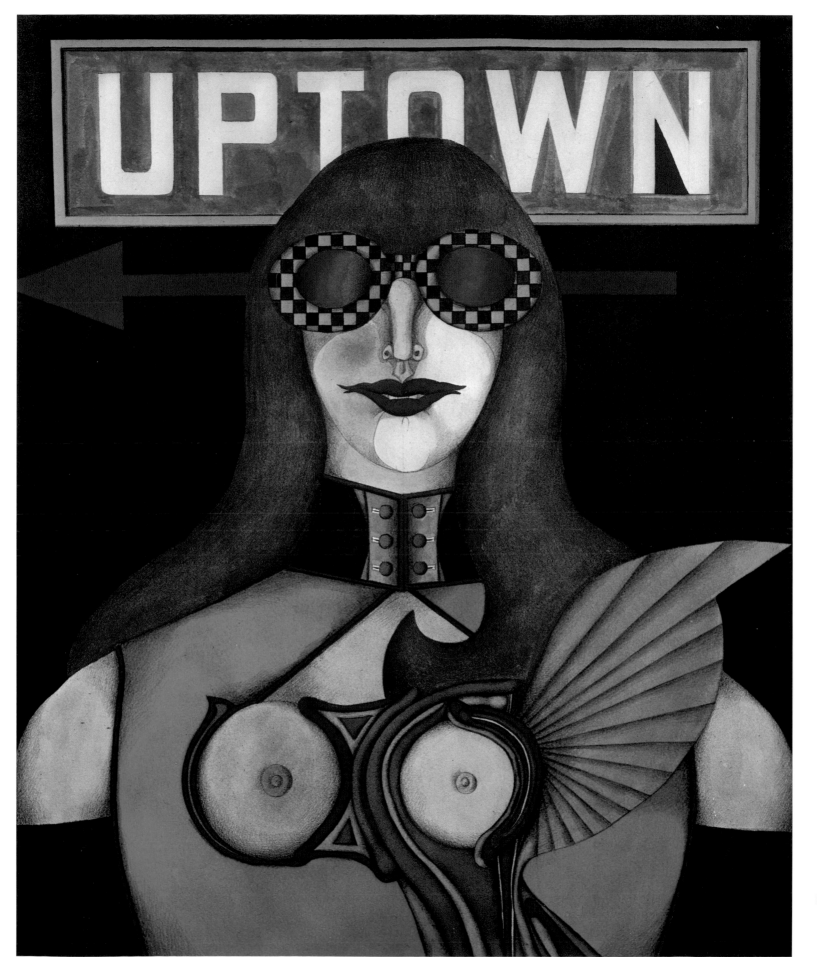

83

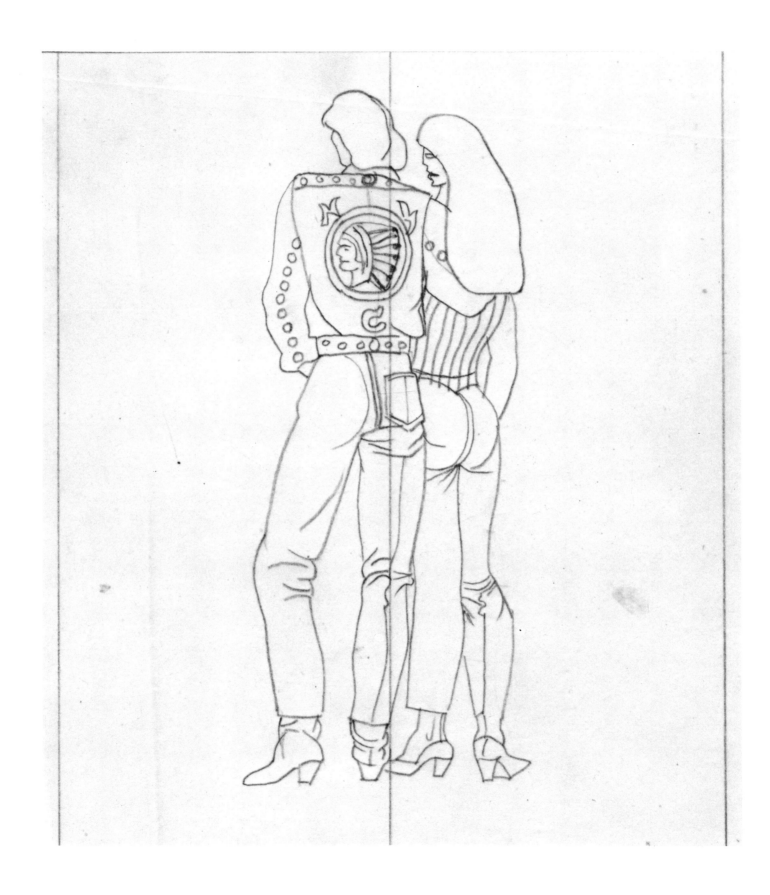

SHOOT, 1969, w/p, 24 × 20 in., 60 × 50 cm. Priv. Coll.

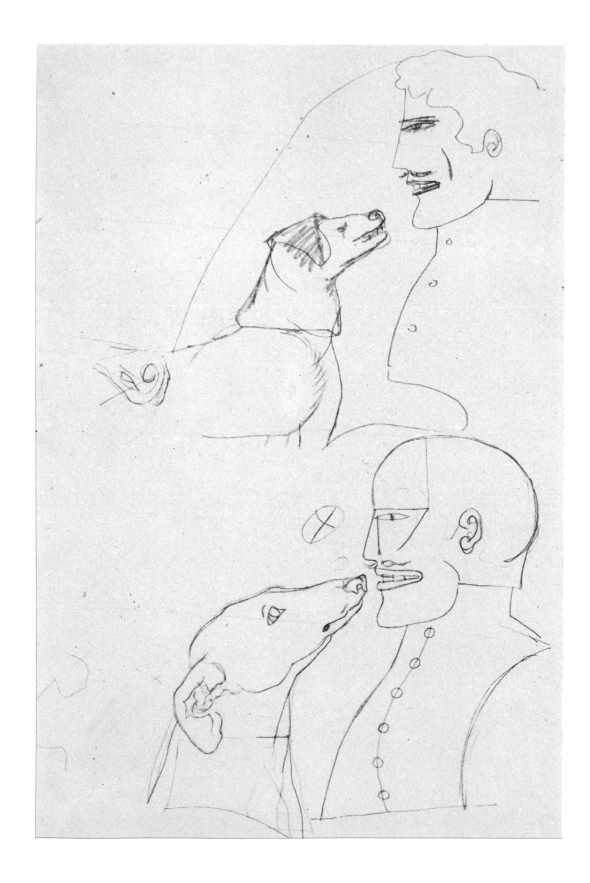

87

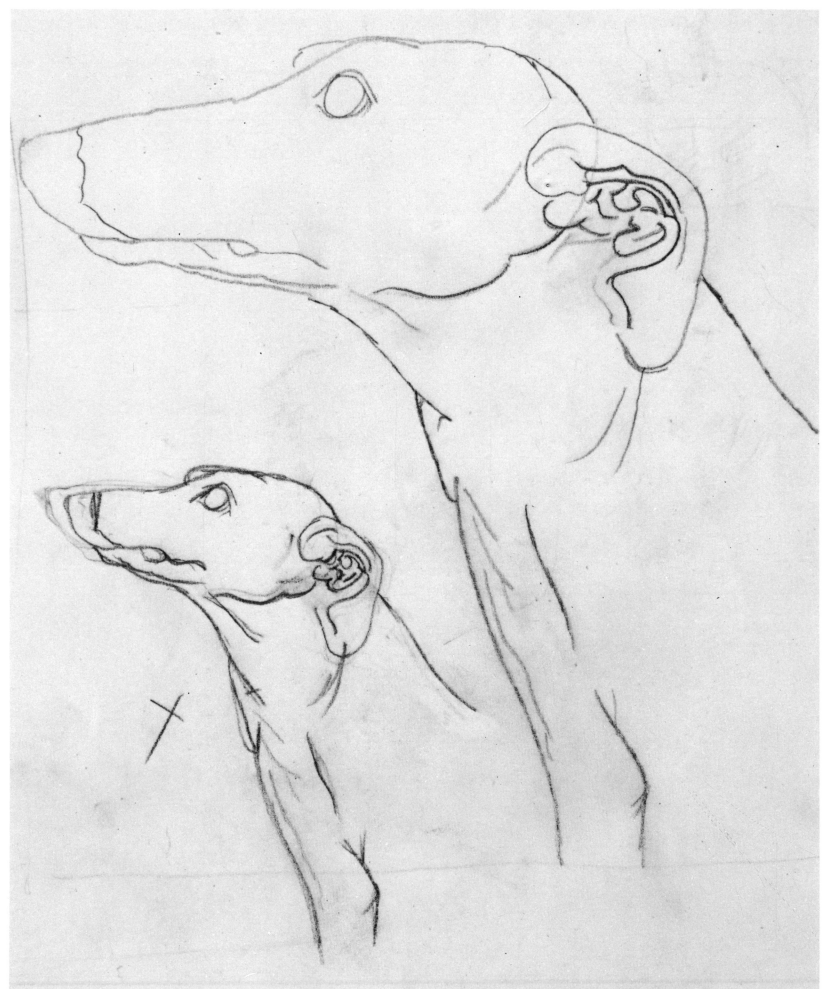

89

91

A MAN'S BEST FRIEND, 1969
w/p, 24 × 20 in., 61 × 51 cm.
Priv. Coll.

R. LINDNER/61

COUPLE I, 1969, w/p, 24 × 20 in., 61 × 51 cm. Galerie Claude Bernard, Paris

LOLLIPOP, ca. 1969
w/p, 24 × 20 in., 61 × 51 cm.
Priv. Coll.

PILLOW AND ALMOST A CIRCLE, 1969
w/p, 24 × 20 in., 61 × 51 cm.
Coll. William Zierler,
New York

100

103

HOW IT ALL BEGAN, 1969
w/p, 24 × 20 in., 61 × 51 cm.
Coll. Sam Shore, New York

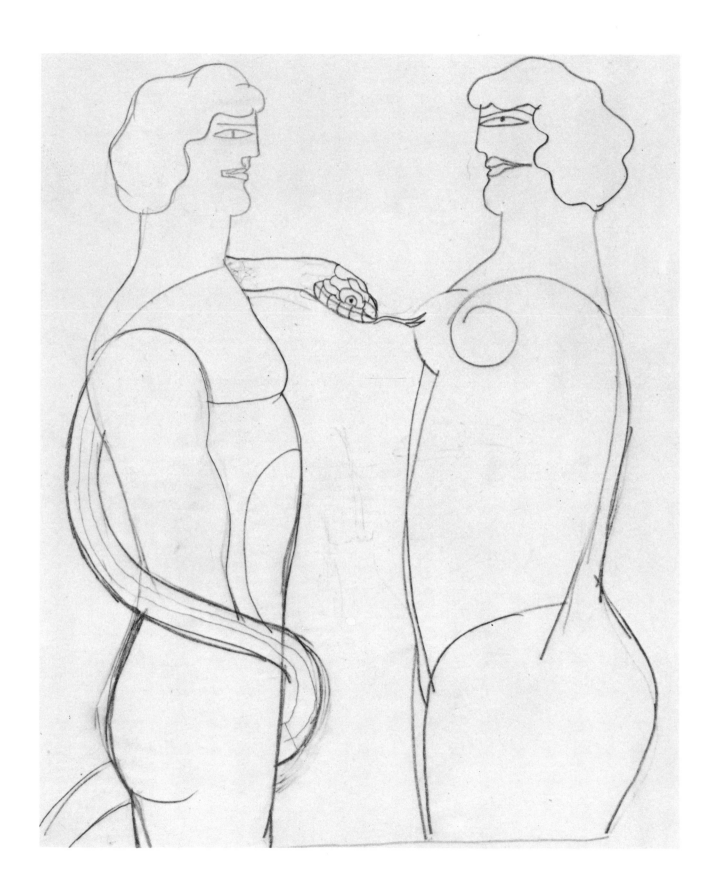

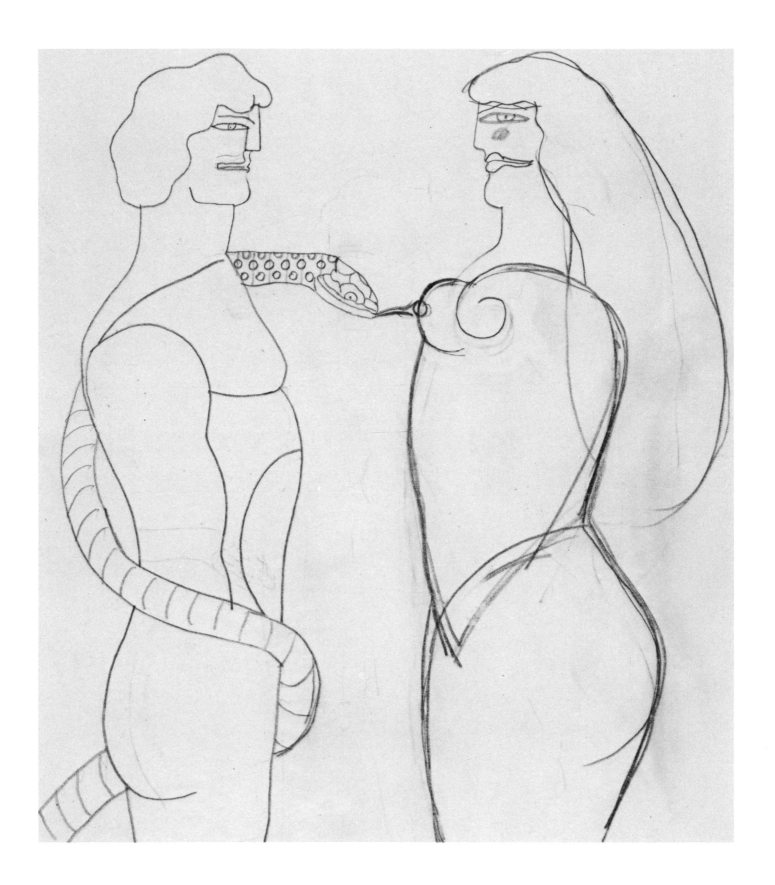

THE HEART, 1969
w/p, 24 × 20 in., 61 × 51 cm.
Galerie Claude Bernard, Paris

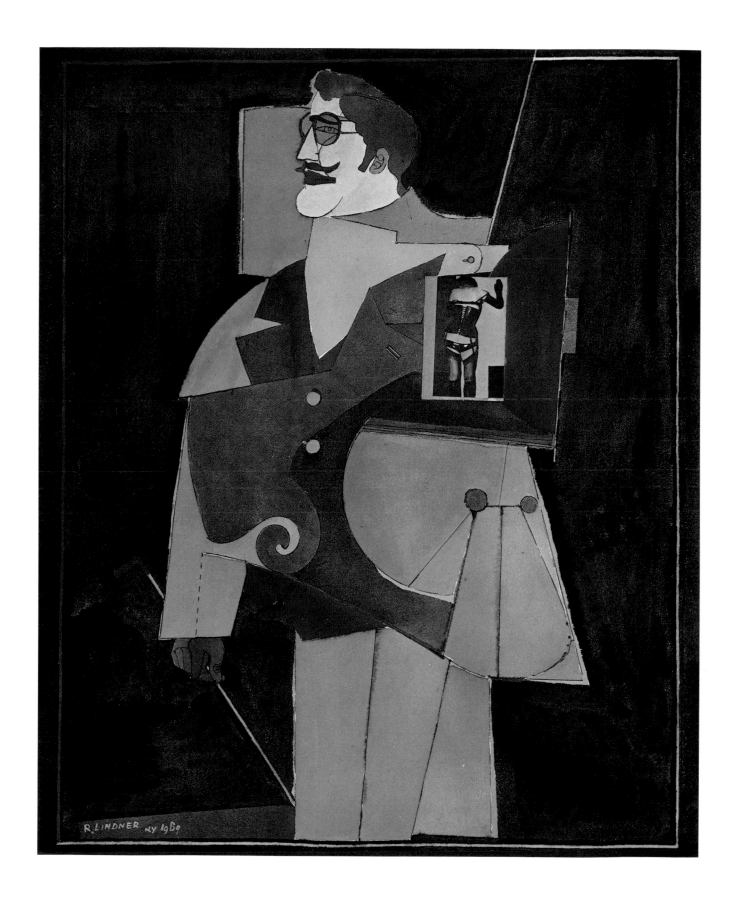

COUPLE II, 1969
w/p, 24 × 20 in., 61 × 51 cm.
Galerie Claude Bernard, Paris

111

115

PROFILE, 1969
w/p, 24 × 20 in., 61 × 51 cm.
Priv. Coll.

117

KISS, 1969, w/p, 24 × 20 in., 61 × 51 cm. Priv. Coll.

TWO, 1969
c/p/c/p, 68 × 58 in., 172 × 149 cm.
Coll. Max Palevsky, Los Angeles

121

123

COUPLE, 1969
w/p, 56 × 46 in., 142 × 117 cm.
Priv. Coll.

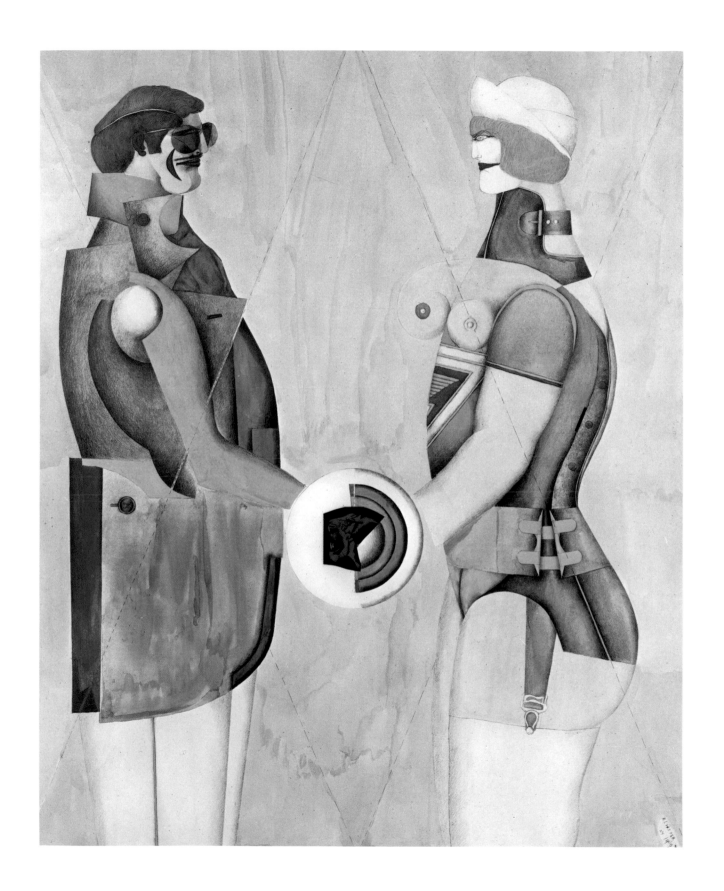

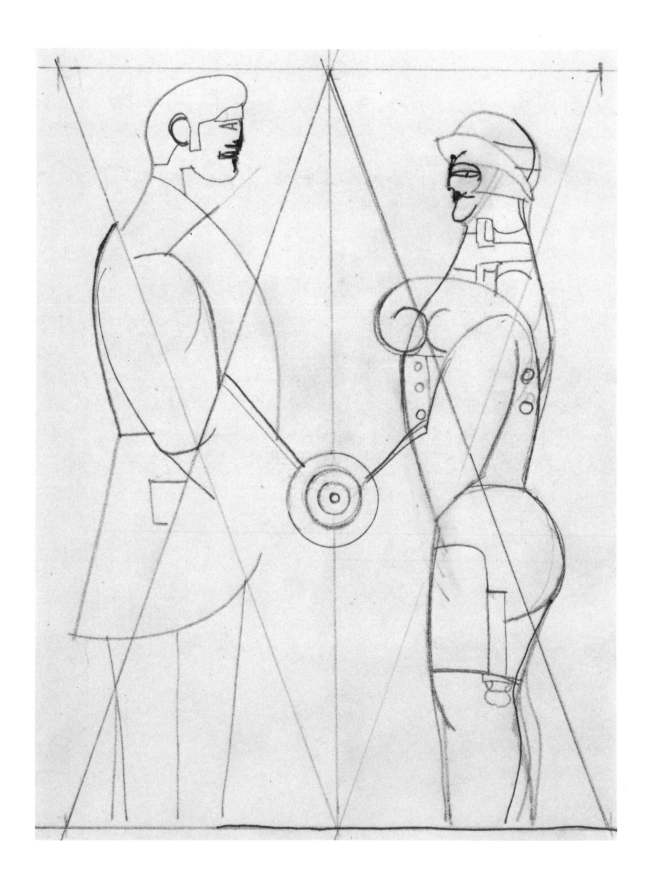

126

127

THE GIFT, 1969
w/p, 27 × 29 in., 70 × 73 cm.
Priv. Coll.

130

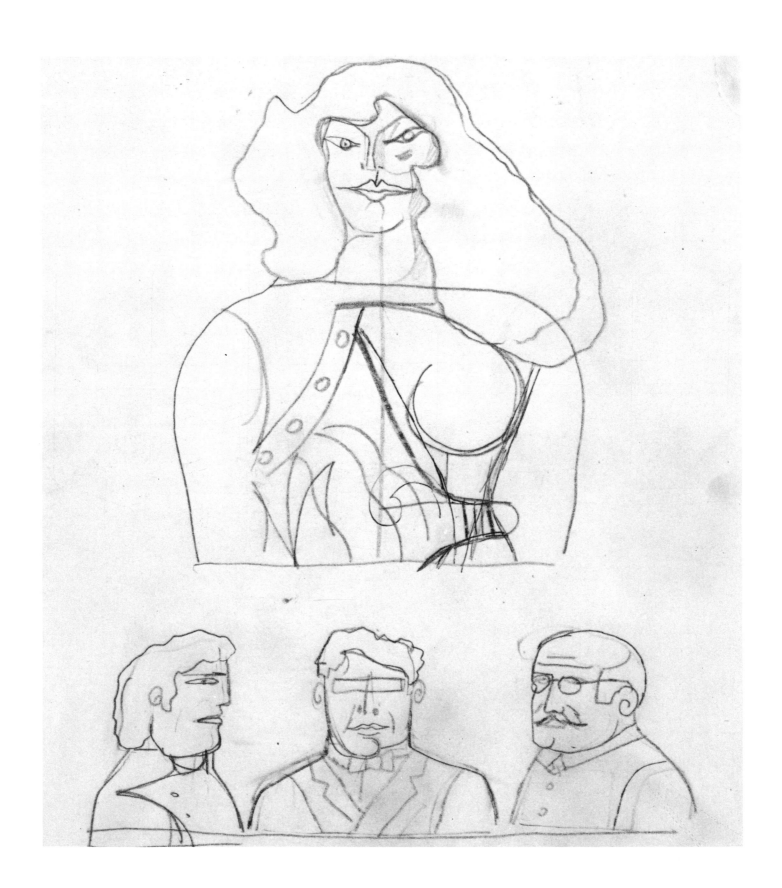

131

THREE UND, 1969
w/p, 67 × 56 in., 170 × 142 cm.
Priv. Coll.

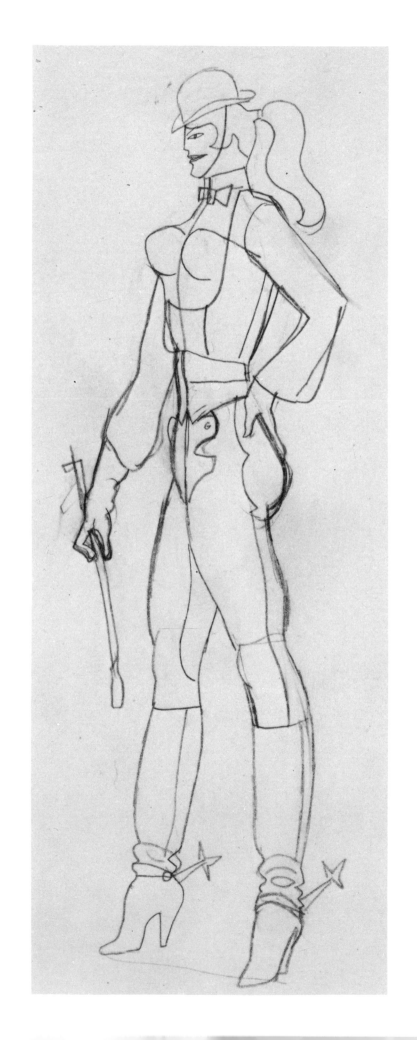

GIRL, 1969
w/c/p, 26 × 15 in., 68 × 36 cm.
Coll. Max Palevsky, Los Angeles

ROOM FOR RENT, 1969
w/p, 41 × 29 in., 104 × 75 cm.
Priv. Coll.

UNTITLED, 1969
w/p, 41 × 29 in., 104 × 74 cm.
Coll. Dr. Glass, New York

TALK TO ME, 1969, w/p, 35 × 27 in., 89 × 69 cm. Priv. Coll.

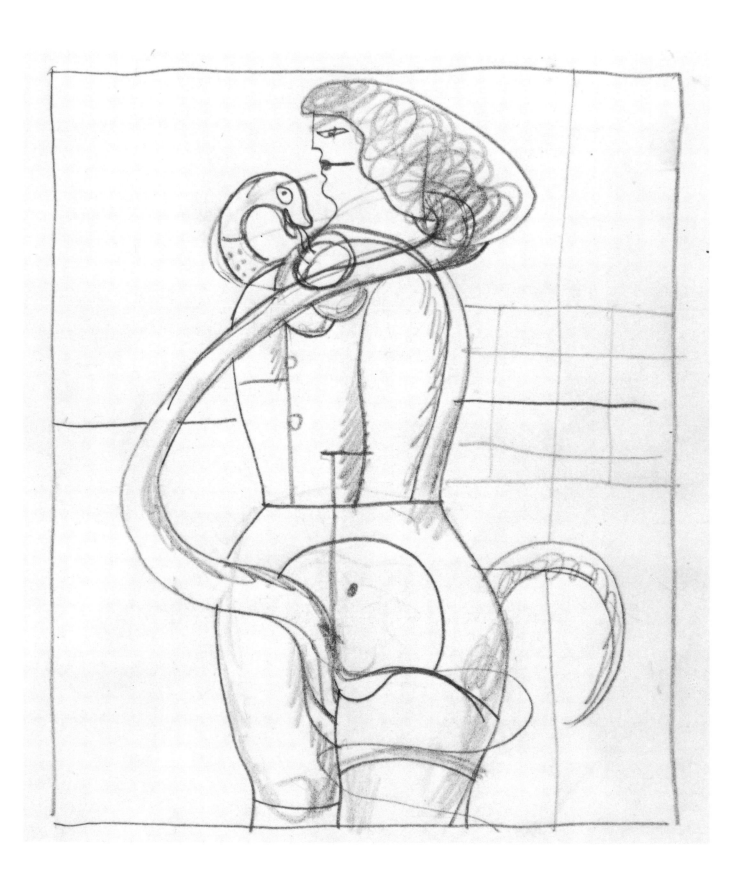

146

147

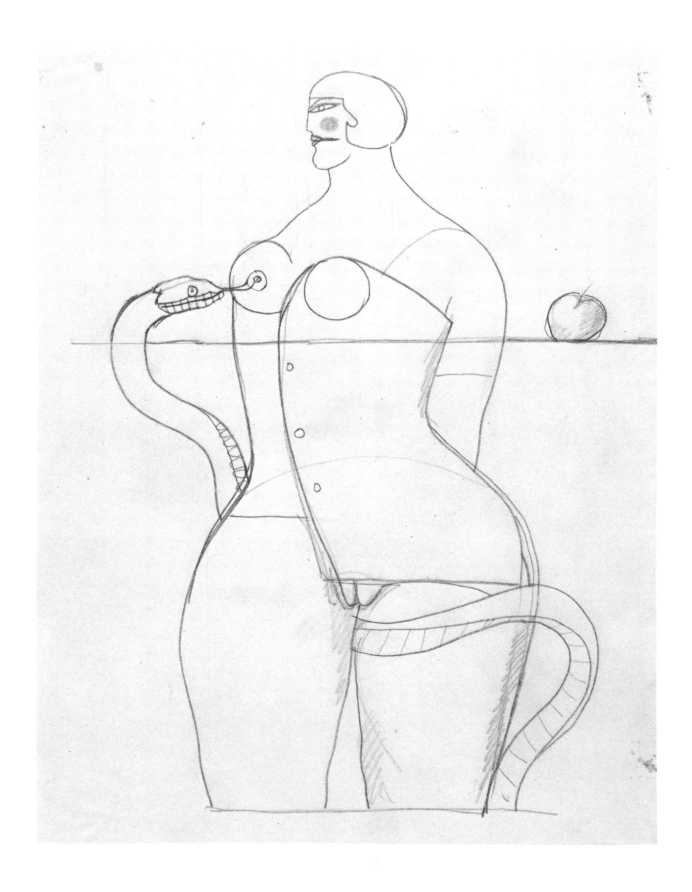

148

KISS NO. 2, 1969, w/p, 40 × 28 in., 102 × 72 cm. Coll. Jacques Kaplan, New York

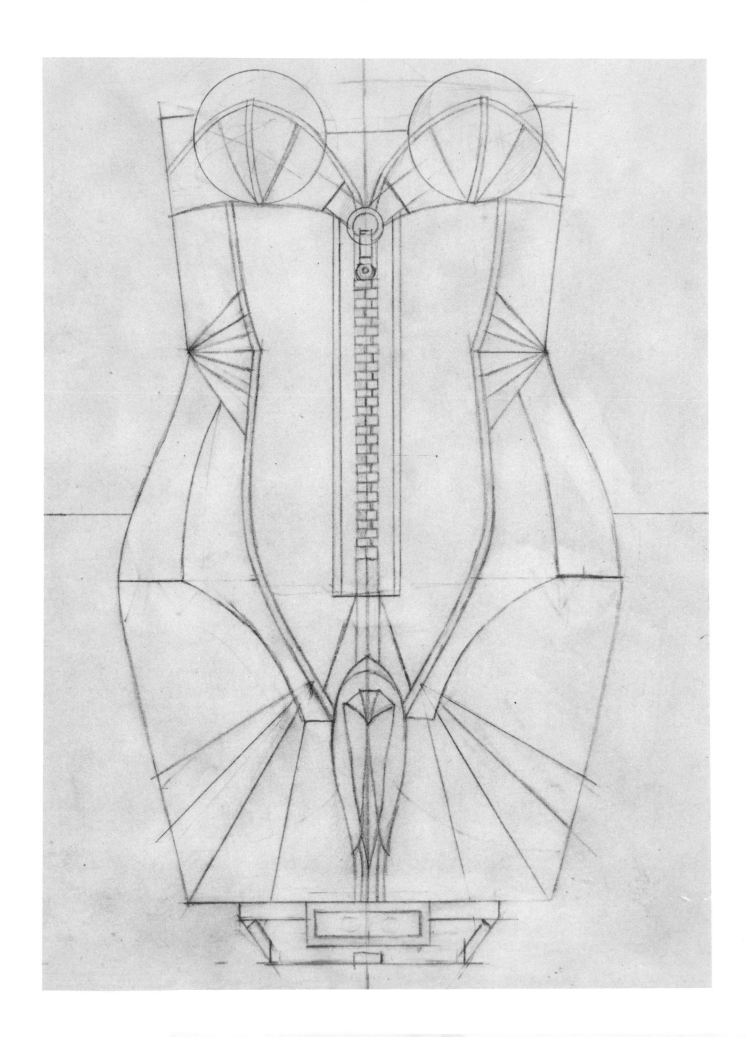

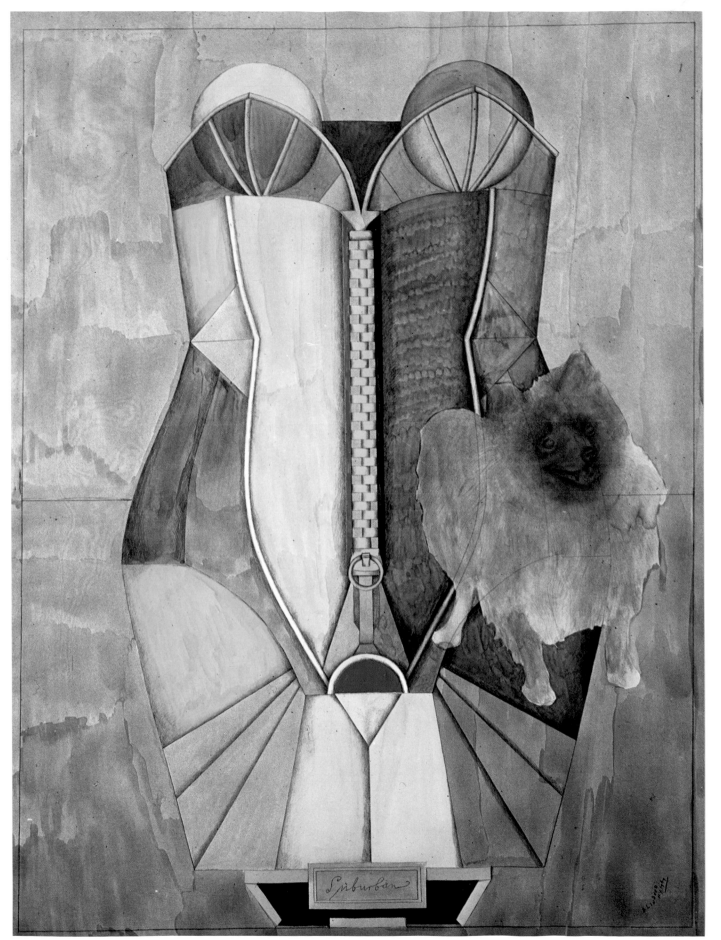

SUBURBAN, 1969, w/p/p, 59×45 in., 150×114 cm. Aberbach Fine Art, New York

TWO PROFILES, 1969, w/p, Priv. Coll.

155

157

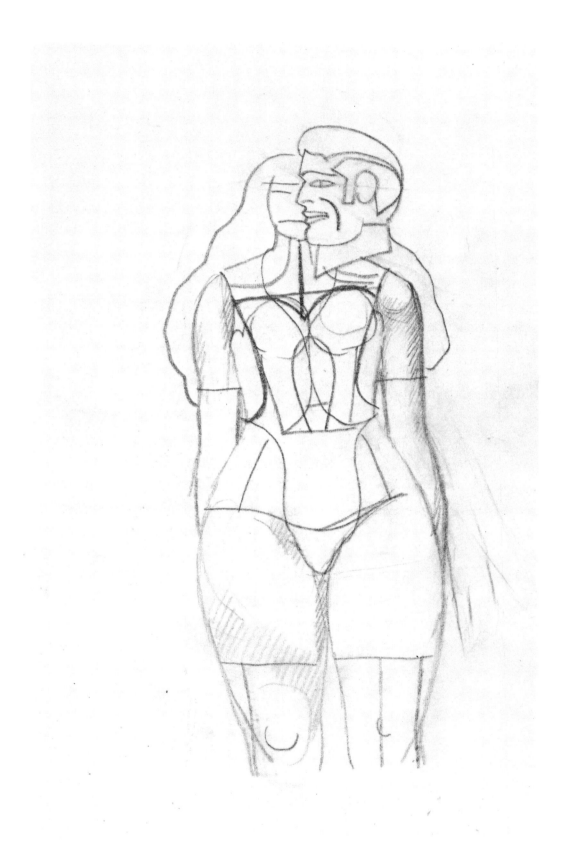

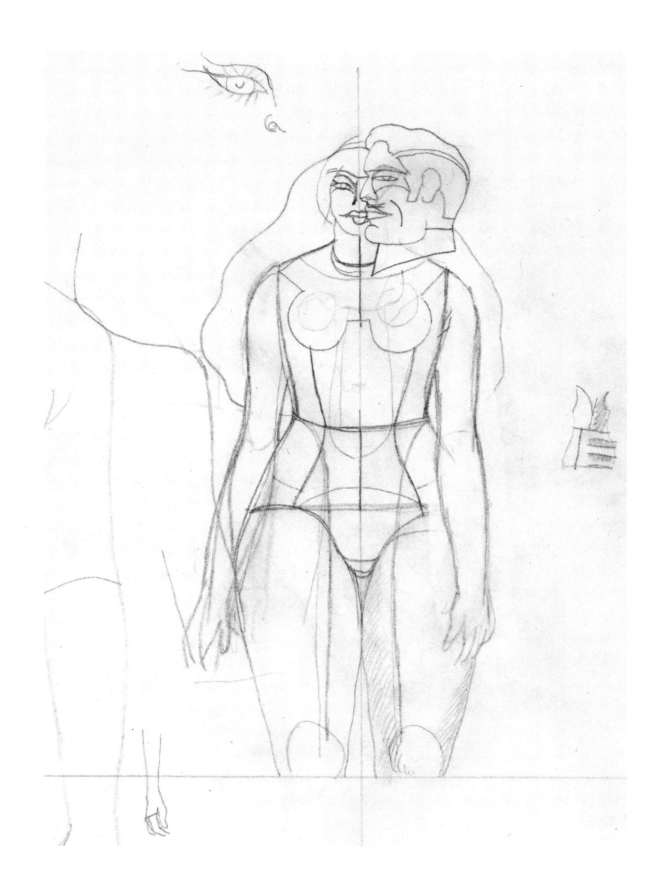

159

WOMAN, 1970
o/c, 75 × 55 in., 191 × 140 cm.
Fischer Fine Art Ltd., London.
Knoedler Gallery, Inc., New York

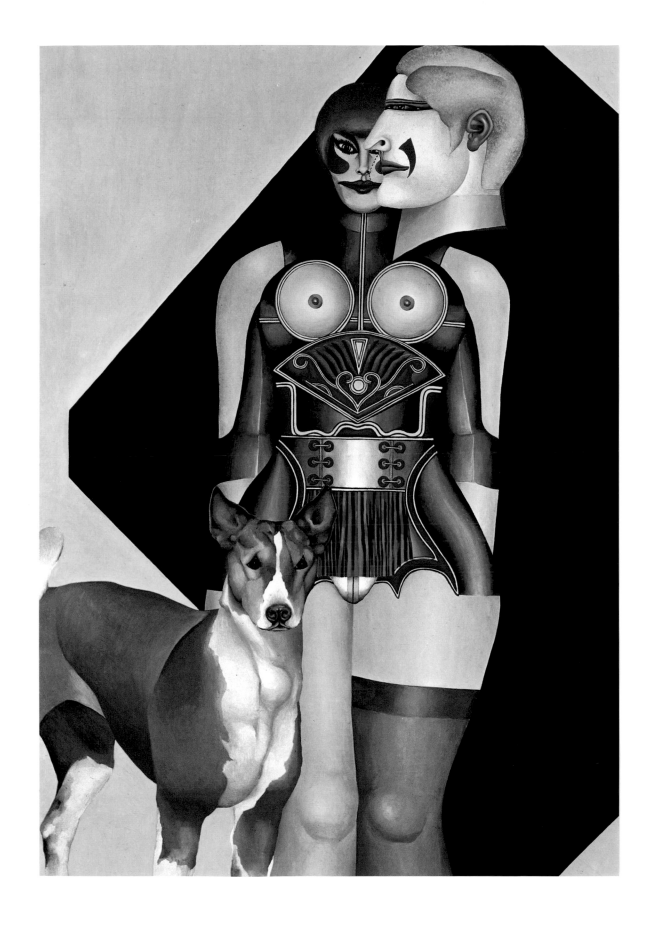

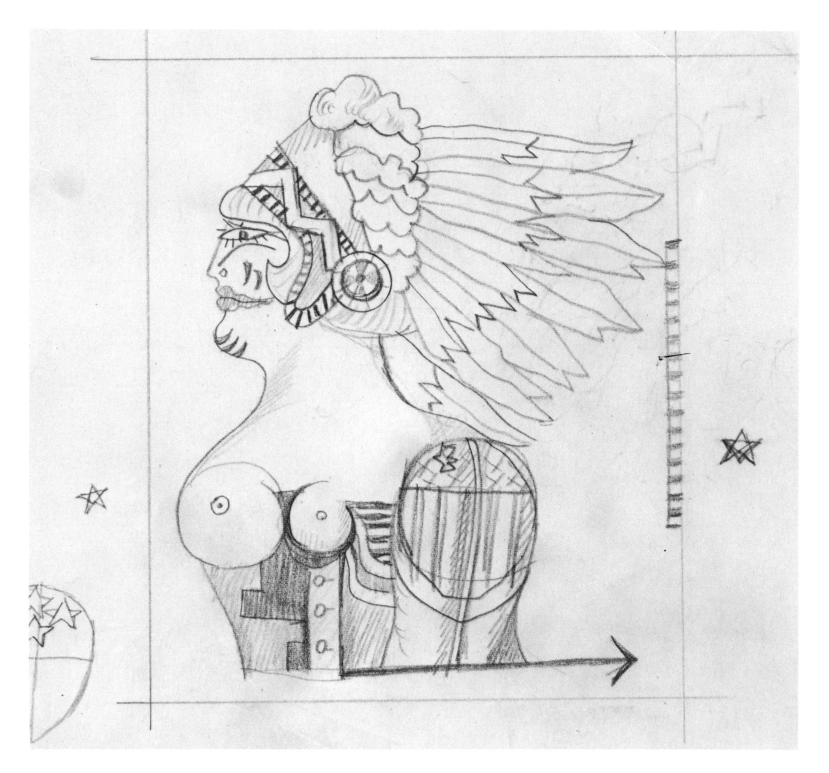

163

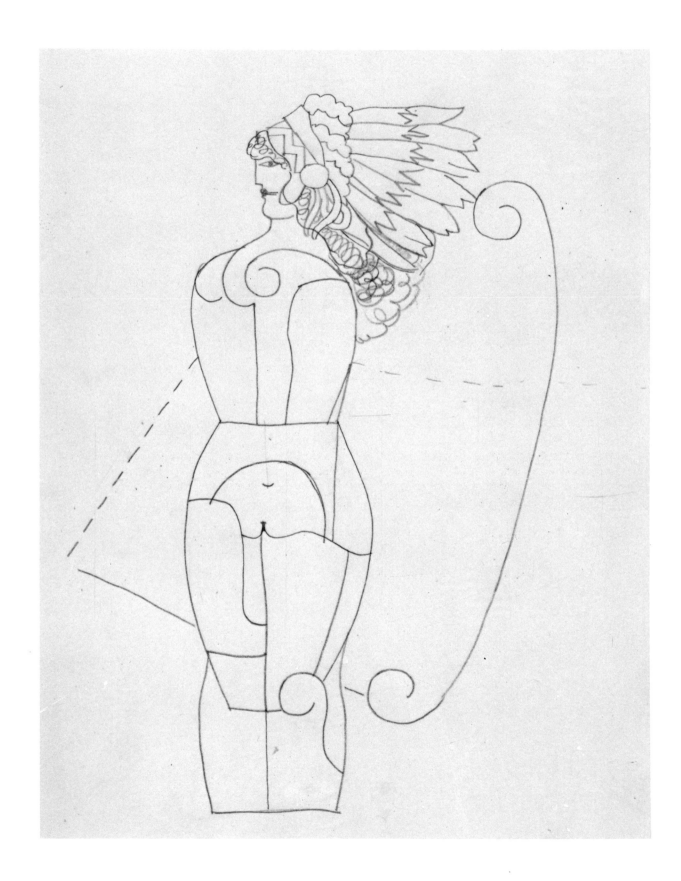

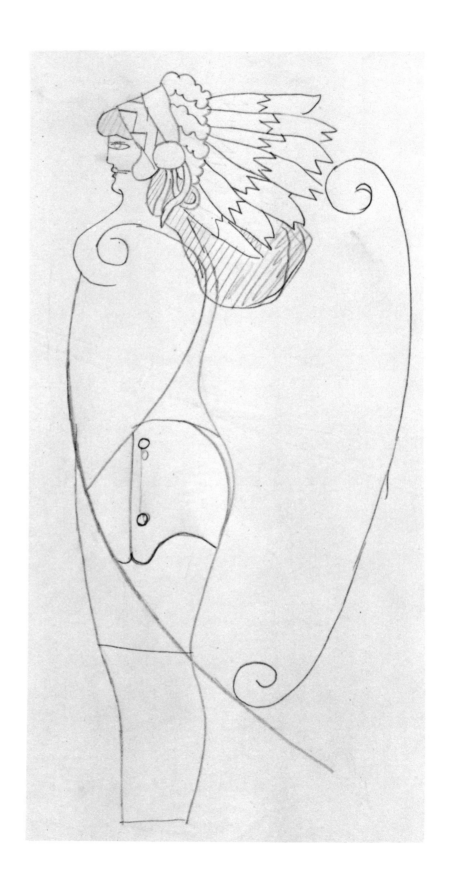

167

MISS AMERICAN INDIAN, 1970
w/p, 24 × 20 in., 61 × 51 cm.
Coll. Sam Shore, New York

THE COUPLE, 1971
o/c, 72 × 78 in., 183 × 198 cm.
Aberbach Fine Art, New York

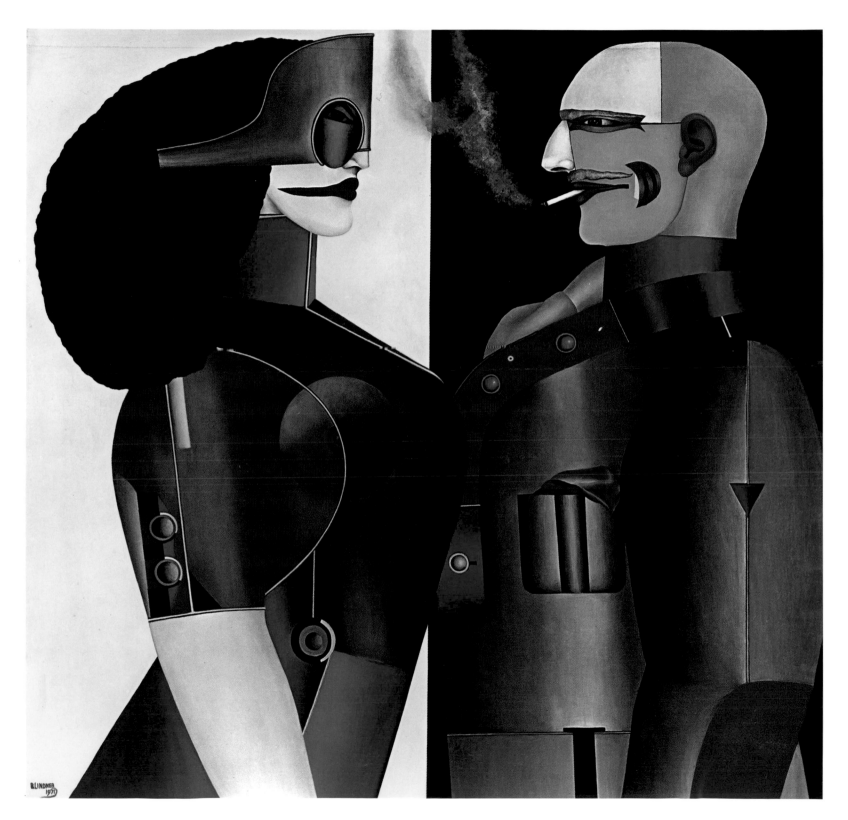

175

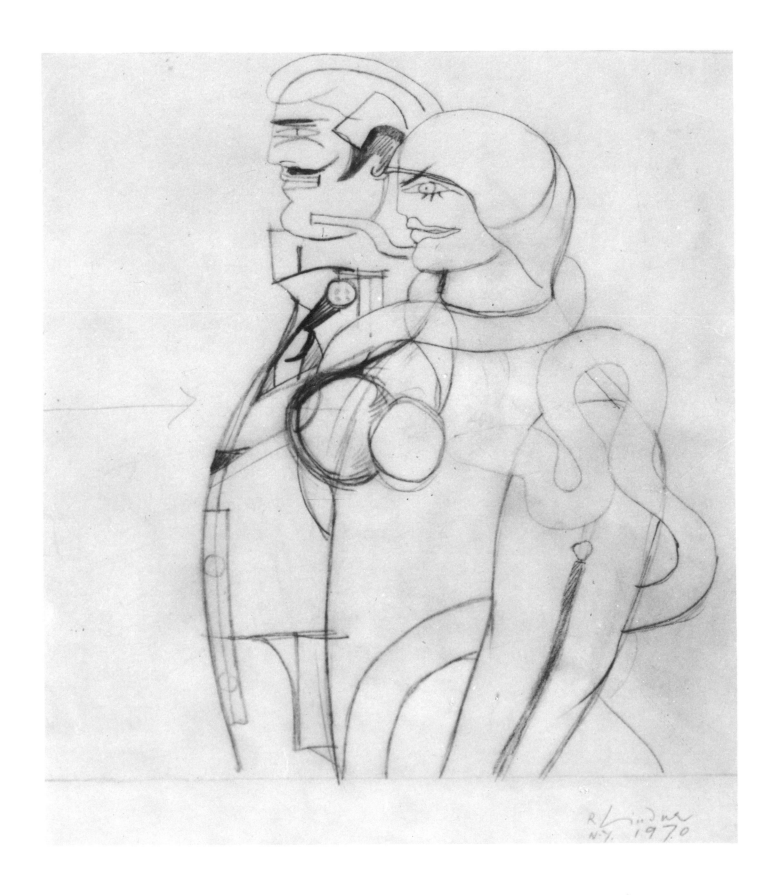

R Lindner
NY 1970

177

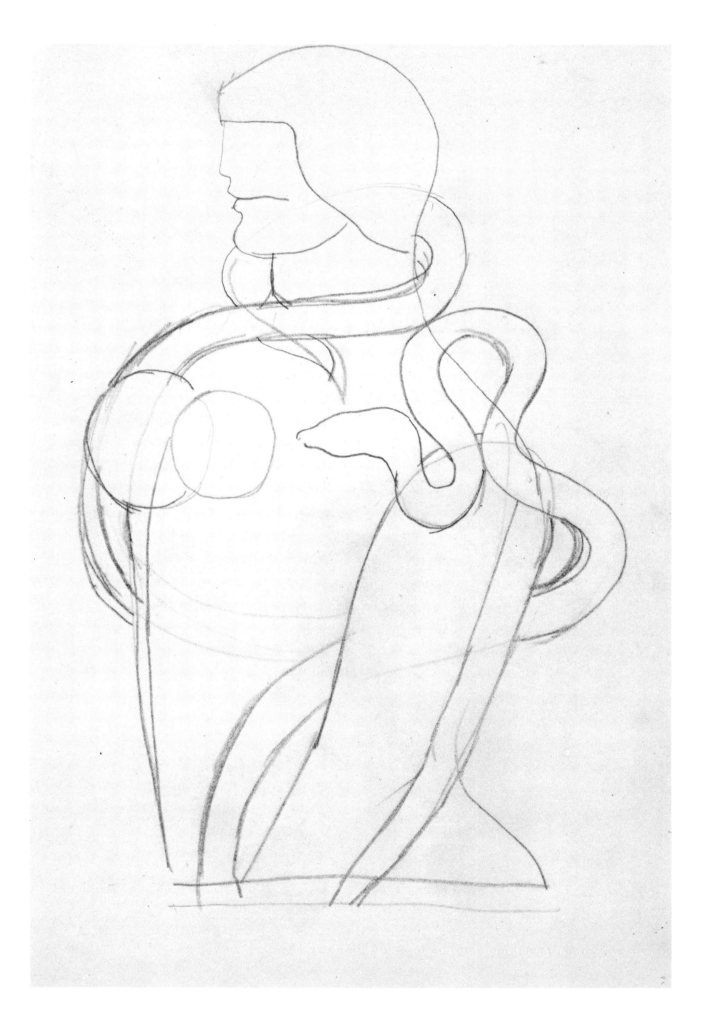

178

AND EVE, 1971
o/c, 72 × 70 in., 183 × 179 cm.
Musée National d'Art Moderne, Paris.
Fonds National d'Art Contemporain

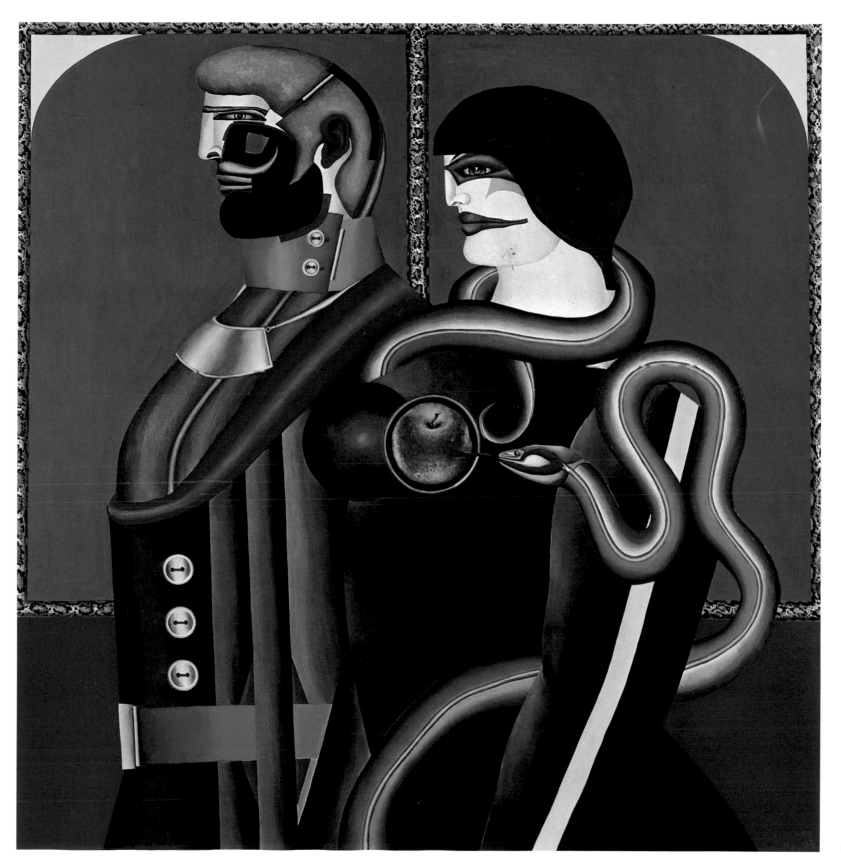

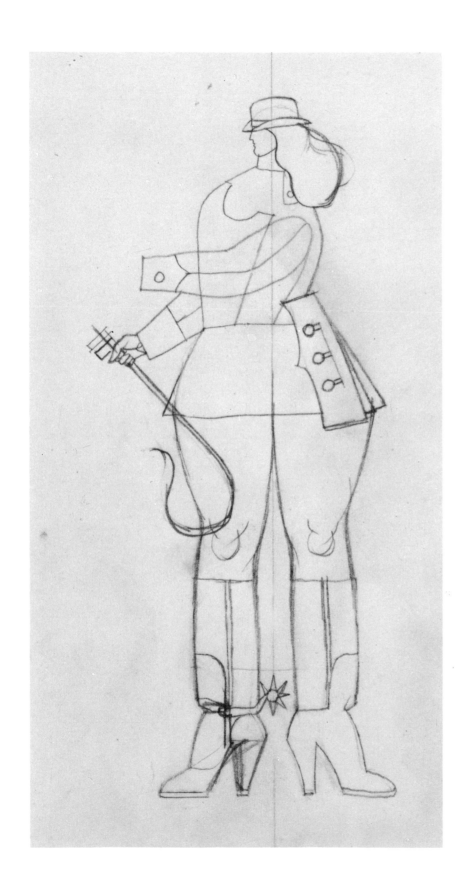

184

THANK YOU, 1971
o/c, 76 × 54 in., 194 × 137 cm.
Galerie Claude Bernard, Paris

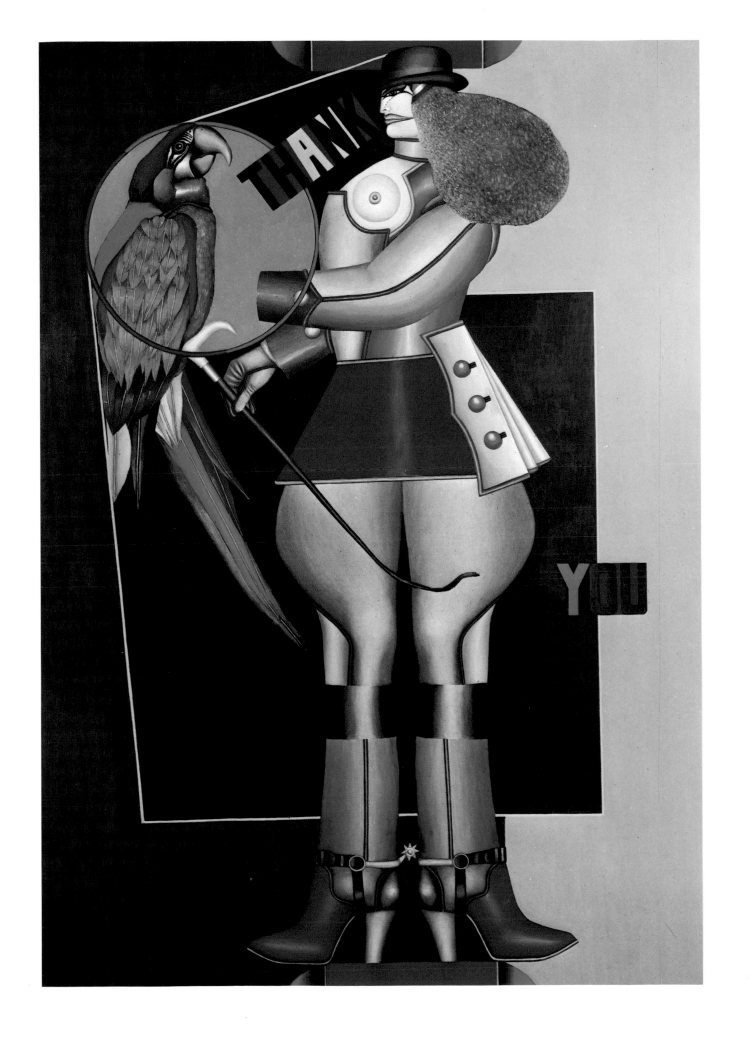

185

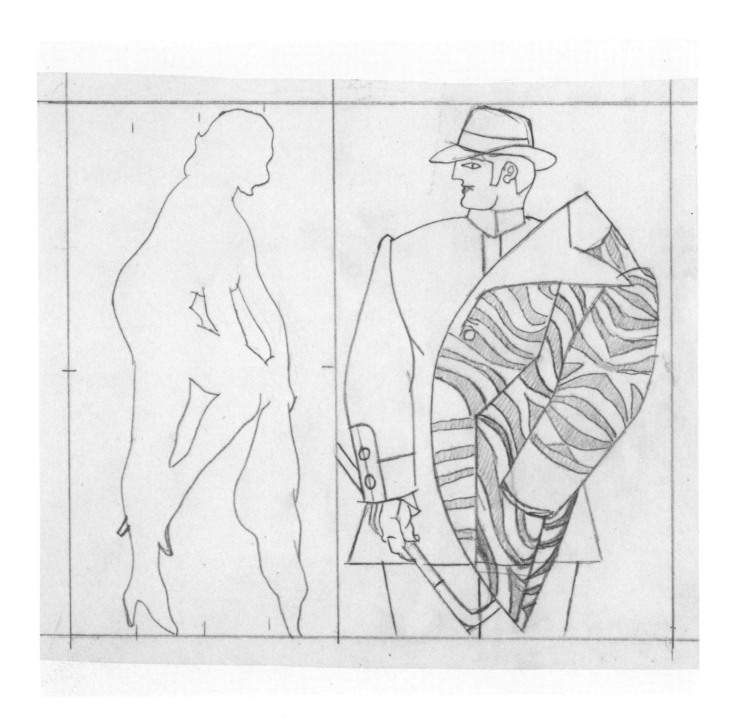

REAR WINDOW, 1971
o/c, 69 × 79 in., 175 × 200 cm.
Priv. Coll.

191

MAN WITH A SWORD, 1971
w/p, 30 × 22 in., 76 × 56 cm.
Priv. Coll.

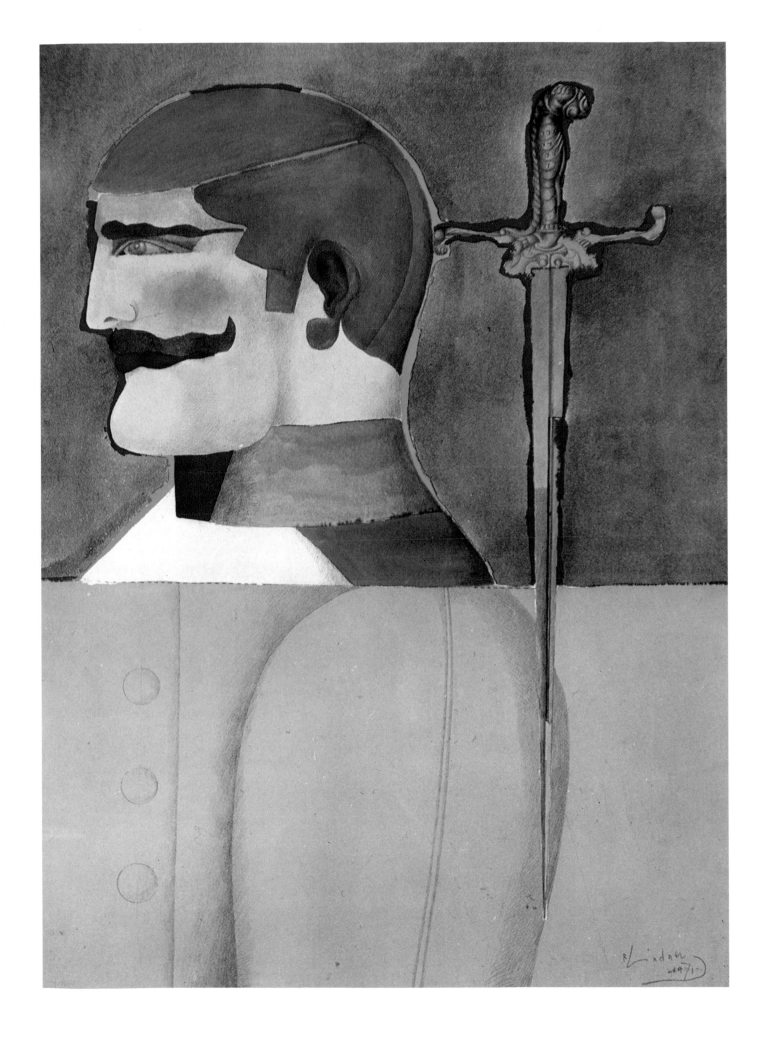

yellow

violet

yellow

PARTNERS, 1971
w/p, 57 × 45 in., 145 × 115 cm.
Coll. Michel Warren, Paris

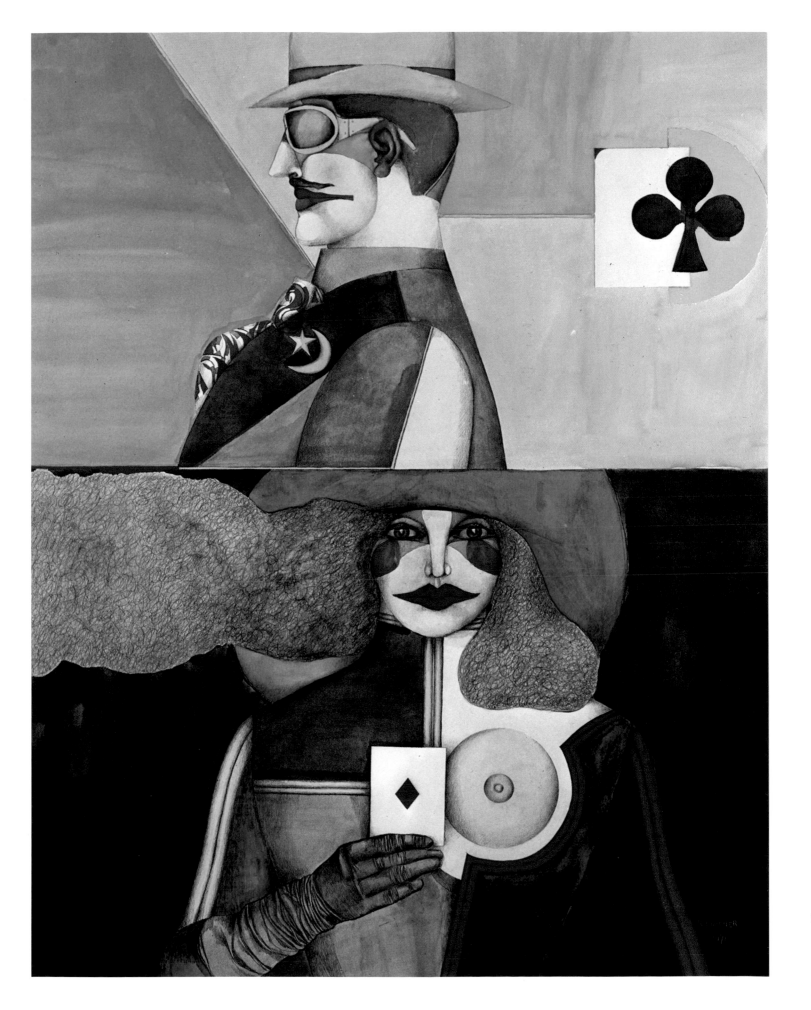

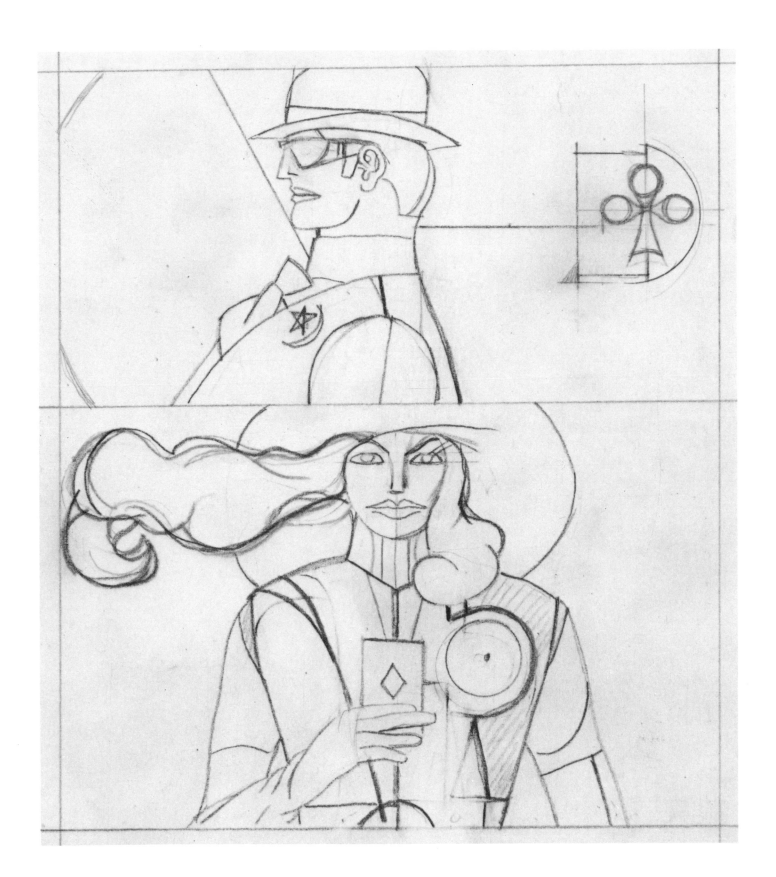

WOMAN ON YELLOW BACKGROUND, 1972
w/p, 26 × 17 in., 65 × 44 cm.
Priv. Coll.

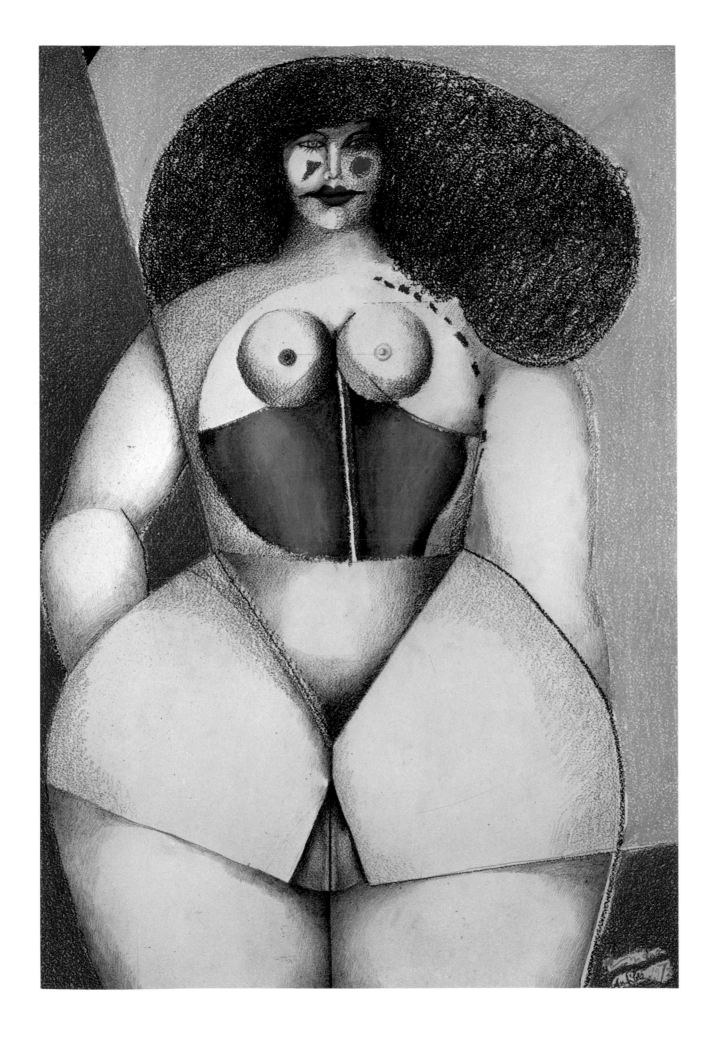

203

GIRL WITH GREEN HAIR, 1972
o/c, 90 × 65 in., 229 × 165 cm.
Fischer Fine Art Ltd., London.
Knoedler Gallery, Inc., New York

CLOUDS, 1972
w/c/p, 30 × 22 in., 76 × 56 cm.
Coll. Michel Warren, Paris

211

213

EAST 69TH STREET, 1972
o/c, 69 × 79 in., 200 × 175 cm.
Museum Boymans van Beuningen, Rotterdam

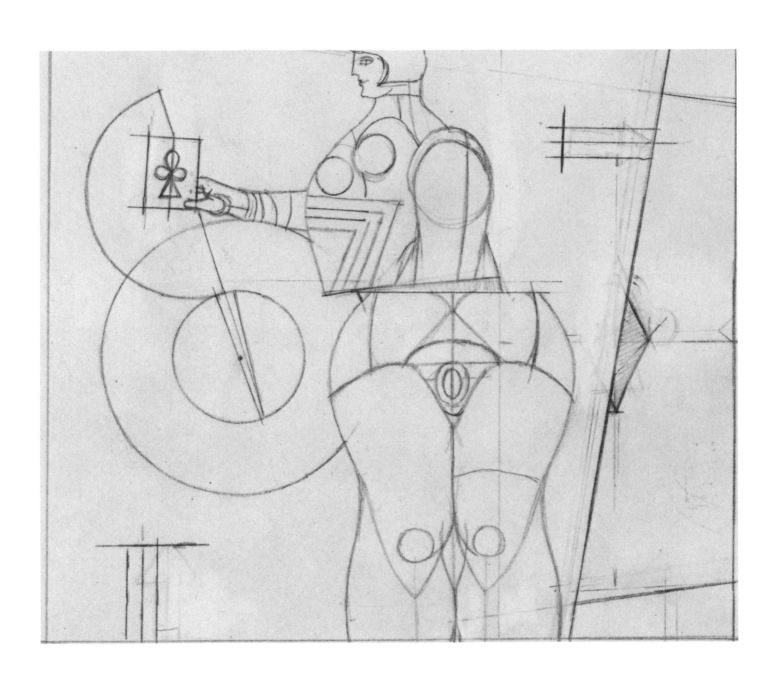

SOLITAIRE, 1973
o/c, 71 × 79 in., 180 × 200 cm.
Fischer Fine Art Ltd., London.
Knoedler Gallery, Inc., New York

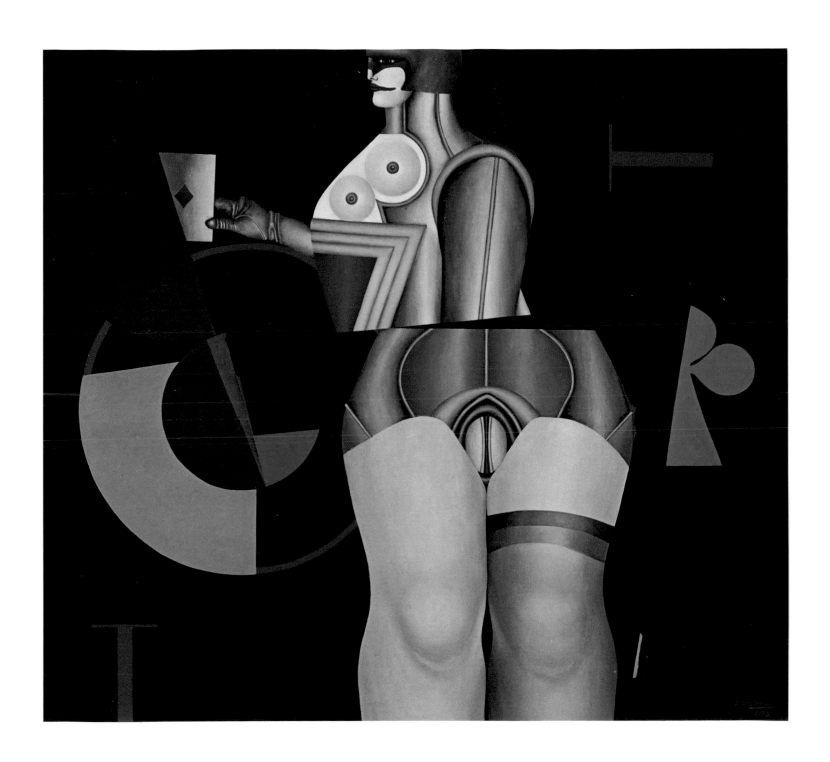

221

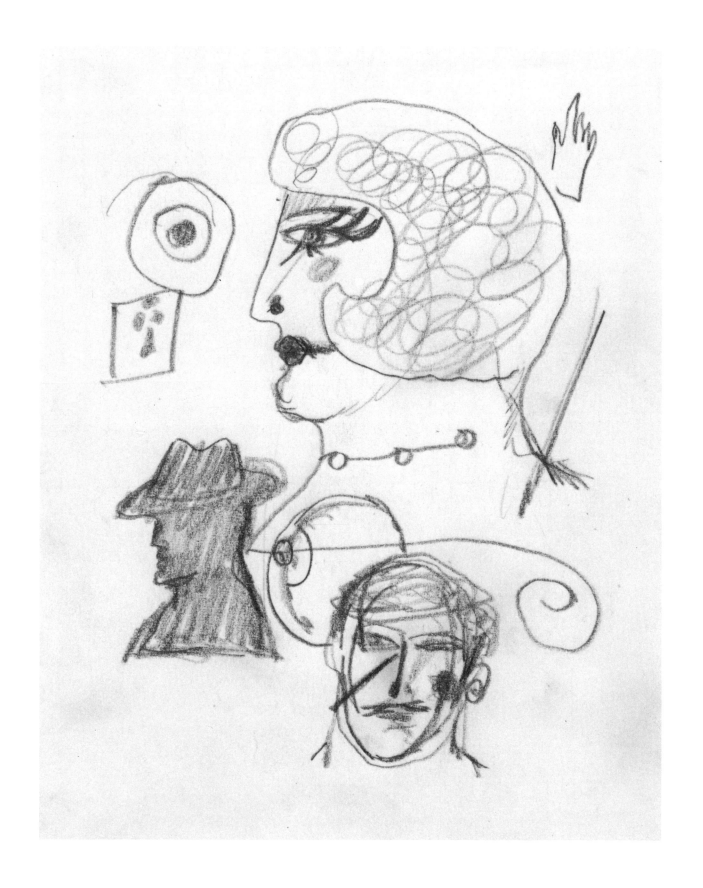

225

CIRCUS, CIRCUS, 1973, o/c, 80 × 70 in., 203 × 178 cm. Coll. Denise Lindner, New York

L'AS DE TRÈFLE, 1973
o/c, 79 × 71 in., 200 × 180 cm.
Priv. Coll.

229

231

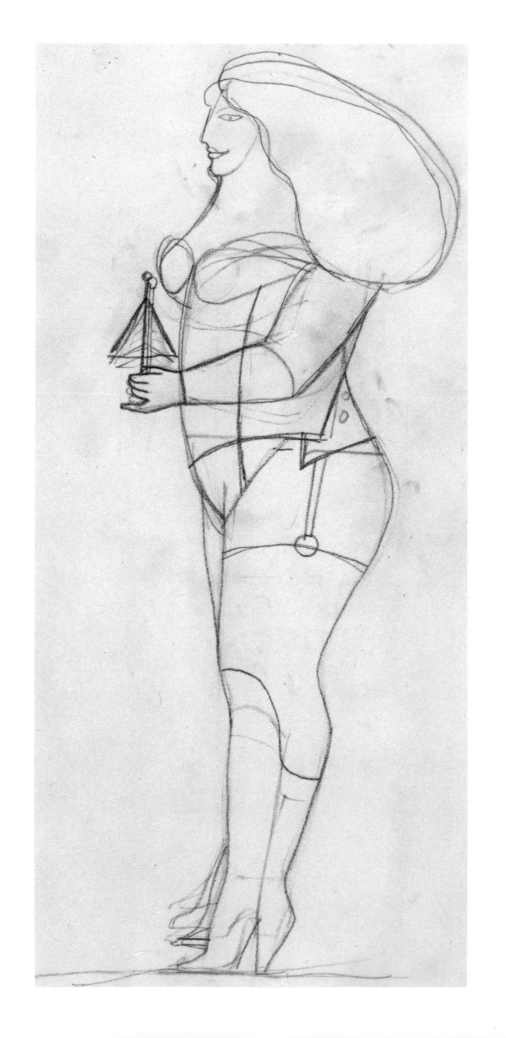

UNTITLED, 1973
w/p, 17 × 13 in., 43 × 33 cm.
Coll. Henri Cartier-Bresson, Paris

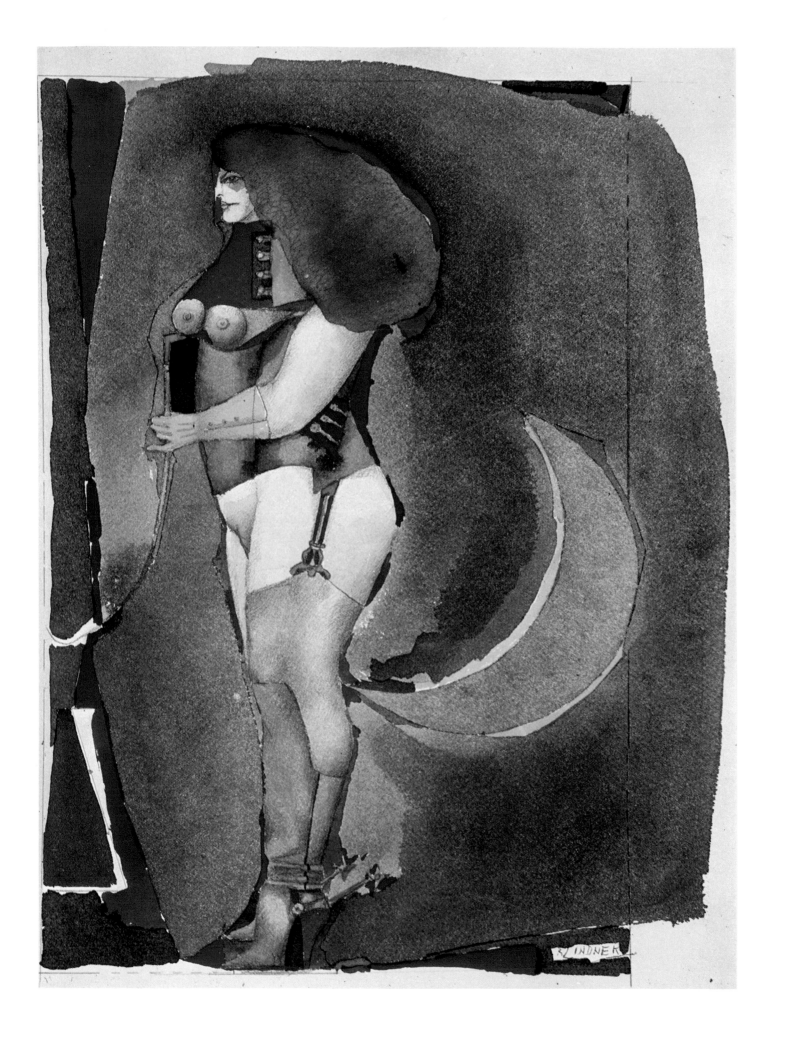

233

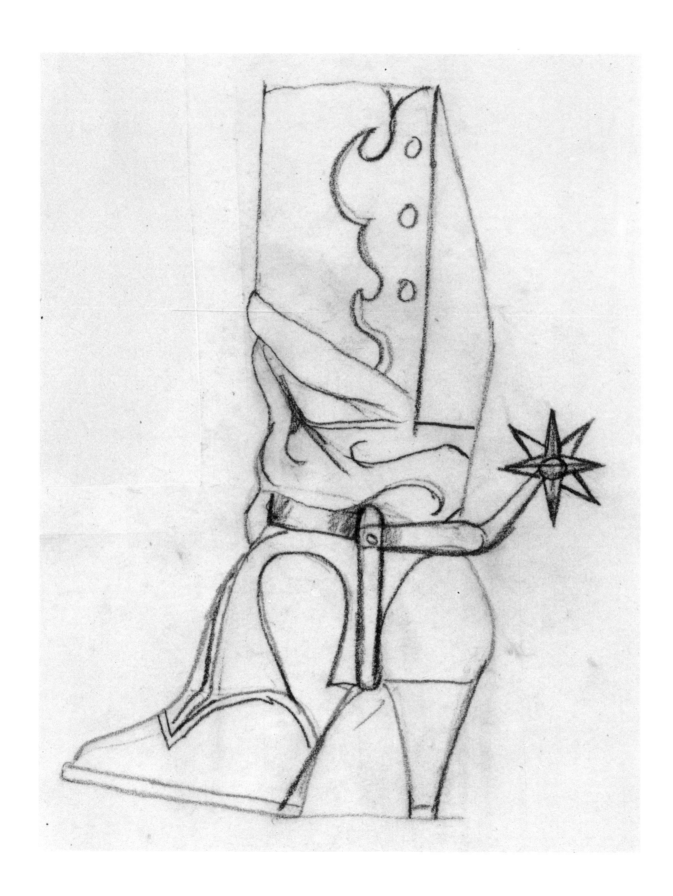

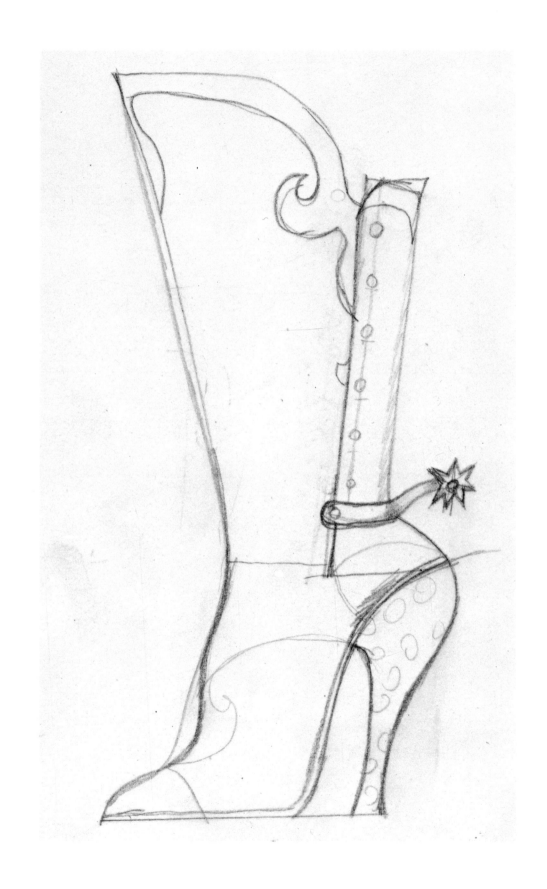

235

TÊTE D'HOMME, 1973
w/p, 27 × 19 in., 68 × 49 cm.
Musée National d'Art Moderne, Paris.
Fonds National d'Art Contemporain

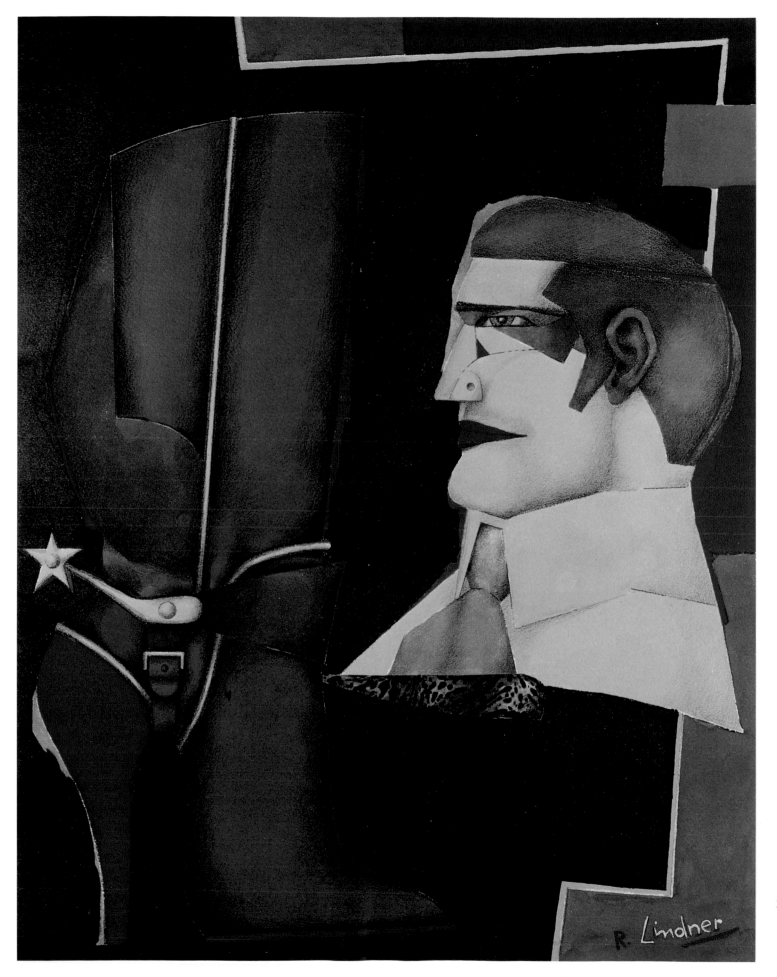

237

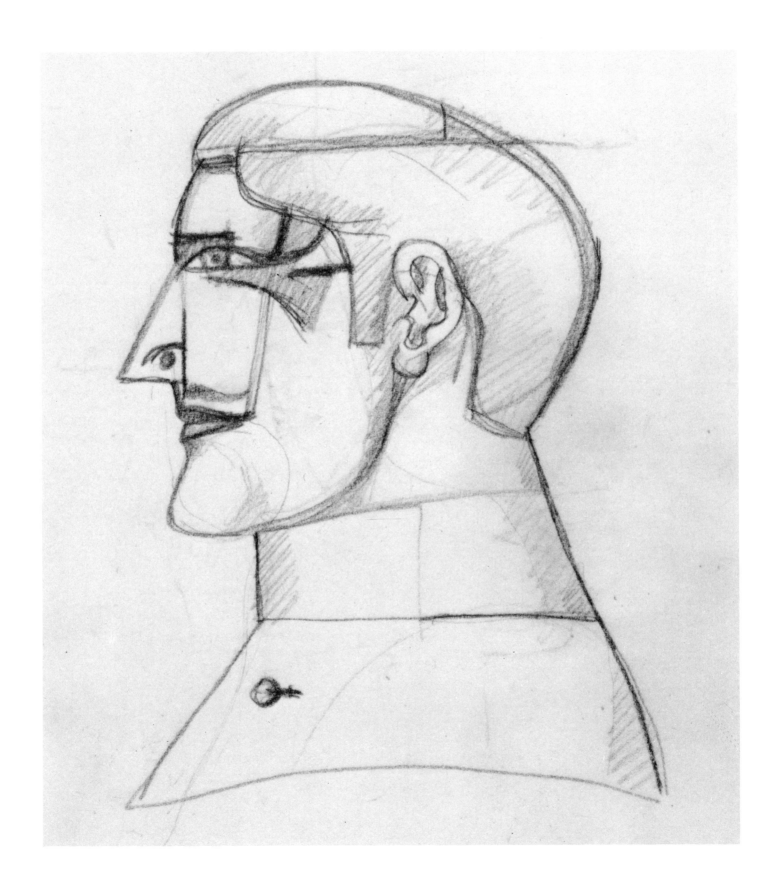

239

GIRL WITH BIRD, 1973
w/p, 12 × 9 in., 31 × 24 cm.
Priv. Coll.

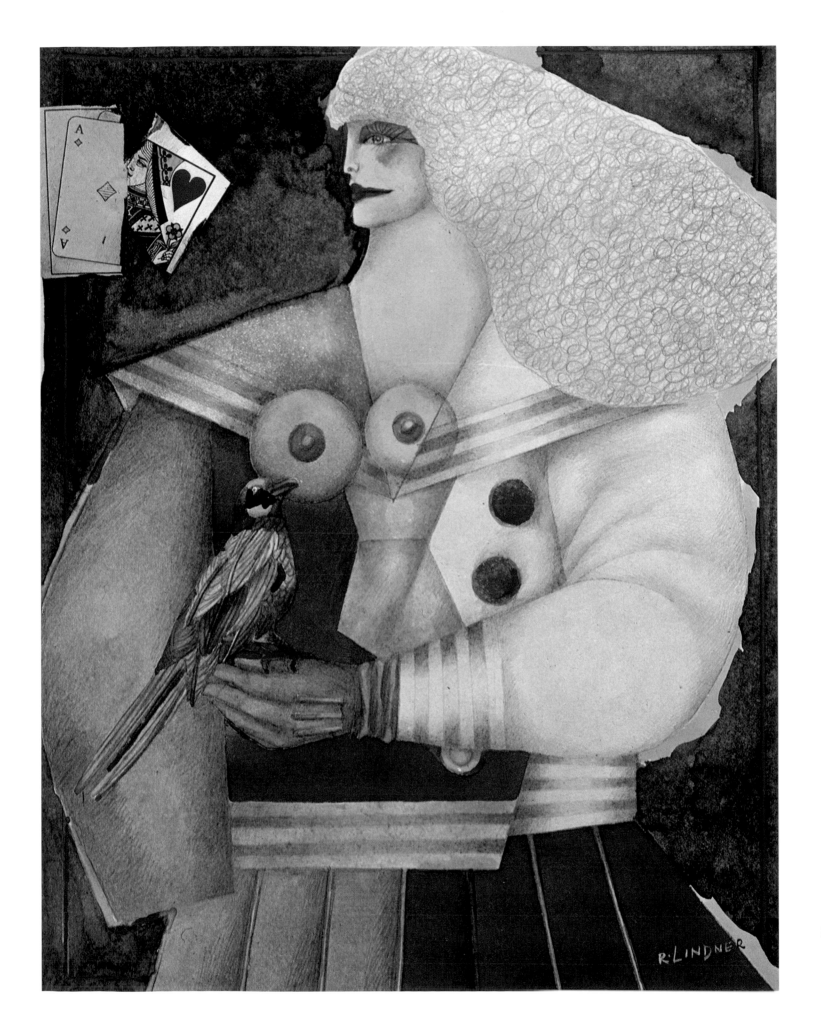

Paintings and Watercolors
Catalogue 1968 to 1974

1968
WATERCOLORS

1. NEW YORK MEN
24 × 20 in., 61 × 51 cm.
Galerie Claude Bernard, Paris

2. ON
24 × 20 in., 61 × 51 cm.
Spencer Samuels and Co., New York

3. FIFTH AVENUE
24 × 20 in., 60 × 51 cm.
Coll. William Zierler, New York

4. OUT OF TOWNERS
24 × 20 in., 61 × 51 cm.
Private collection

5. 24 HOUR SELF-SERVICE
24 × 20 in., 61 × 51 cm.
Coll. Playboy Enterprises, New York

6. FIRST AVENUE
24 × 20 in., 61 × 51 cm.
Galerie Beyeler, Basel

7. ARTURO UI
30 × 20 in., 76 × 51 cm.
Coll. Rhode Island School of Design,
Providence, Rhode Island

8. TO SASHA
16 × 11 in., 39 × 28 cm.
Coll. Alexander Schneider, New York

9. POET (PORTRAIT OF GINZBURG)
24 × 20 in., 61 × 51 cm.
Knoedler Gallery, Inc., New York

1969
WATERCOLORS

1. FUN CITY
27 × 40 in., 69 × 102 cm.
Coll. Hal Reed, New York

2. GIRL WITH HOOP
24 × 20 in., 61 × 51 cm.
Private collection

3. SHOOT
24 × 20 in., 60 × 51 cm.
Private collection

4. UPTOWN
24 × 20 in., 61 × 51 cm.
Coll. Sam Shore, New York

5. ST. MARK'S PLACE
24 × 20 in., 61 × 51 cm.
Coll. Hal Reed, New York

6. HIT
24 × 20 in., 61 × 51 cm.
Spencer Samuels and Co., New York

7. LOLLIPOP
24 × 20 in., 61 × 51 cm.
Private collection

8. A MAN'S BEST FRIEND
24 × 20 in., 61 × 51 cm.
Private collection

9. COUPLE I
24 × 20 in., 61 × 51 cm.
Galerie Claude Bernard, Paris

10. PILLOW AND ALMOST A CIRCLE
24 × 20 in., 61 × 51 cm.
Coll. William Zierler, New York

11. HOW IT ALL BEGAN
24 × 20 in., 61 × 51 cm.
Coll. Sam Shore, New York

12. COUPLE II
24 × 20 in., 61 × 51 cm.
Galerie Claude Bernard, Paris

13. THE HEART
24 × 20 in., 61 × 51 cm.
Galerie Claude Bernard, Paris

14. PROFILE
24 × 20 in., 61 × 51 cm.
Private collection

15. KISS
24 × 20 in., 61 × 51 cm.
Private collection

16. SHOOT I
41 × 29 in., 104 × 74 cm.
Galerie Claude Bernard, Paris

17. SHOOT II
41 × 29 in., 104 × 74 cm.
Galerie Claude Bernard, Paris

18. SHOOT III
41 × 29 in., 104 × 74 cm.
Galerie Claude Bernard, Paris

19. COUPLE
56 × 46 in., 142 × 117 cm.
Private collection

20. THREE UND
67 × 56 in., 170 × 142 cm.
Private collection

21. GIRL
26 × 15 in., 68 × 36 cm.
Coll. Max Palevsky, Los Angeles

22. TALK TO ME
35 × 27 in., 89 × 69 cm.
Private collection

CRAYON, PENCIL,
COLLAGE

1970
PAINTINGS,
OIL ON CANVAS

WATERCOLOR

23. SUBURBAN
59 × 45 in., 150 × 114 cm.
Aberbach Fine Art, New York

24. ROOM FOR RENT
41 × 29 in., 104 × 75 cm.
Private collection

25. TWO PROFILES
Private collection

26. KISS No. 2
40 × 28 in., 102 × 72 cm.
Coll. Jacques Kaplan, New York

27. THE GIFT
27 × 29 in., 70 × 73 cm.
Private collection

28. UNTITLED
41 × 29 in., 104 × 74 cm.
Coll. Dr. Glass

29. INDIAN WOMAN
12 × 9 in., 31 × 24 cm.
Private collection

30. TWO
68 × 58 in., 172 × 149 cm.
Coll. Max Palevsky, Los Angeles

1. WOMAN
75 × 55 in., 191 × 140 cm.
Fischer Fine Arts Ltd., London
Knoedler Gallery, Inc., New York

2. PORTRAIT OF JOAN LAPHAM
50 × 40 in., 126 × 102 cm.
Coll. Mrs. Brooke Blake, Dallas

1. MISS AMERICAN INDIAN
24 × 20 in., 61 × 51 cm.
Coll. Sam Shore, New York

1971
PAINTINGS,
OIL ON CANVAS

1. THE COUPLE
72 × 78 in., 183 × 198 cm.
Aberbach Fine Art, New York

2. THANK YOU
76 × 54 in., 194 × 137 cm.
Galerie Claude Bernard, Paris

3. AND EVE
72 × 70 in., 183 × 179 cm.
Musée National d'Art Moderne, Paris
Fonds National d'Art Contemporain

4. REAR WINDOW
69 × 79 in., 175 × 200 cm.
Private collection

WATERCOLORS

1. PARTNERS
57 × 45 in., 145 × 115 cm.
Coll. Michel Warren, Paris

2. MAN WITH A SWORD
30 × 22 in., 76 × 56 cm.
Private collection

1972
PAINTINGS,
OIL ON CANVAS

1. EAST 69TH STREET
69 × 79 in., 200 × 175 cm.
Museum Boymans van Beuningen, Rotterdam

2. GIRL WITH GREEN HAIR
90 × 65 in., 229 × 165 cm.
Fischer Fine Arts Ltd., London
Knoedler Gallery, Inc., New York

WATERCOLOR

1. WOMAN WITH YELLOW BACKGROUND
26 × 17 in., 66 × 44 cm.
Private collection

WATERCOLOR
AND COLLAGE

2. CLOUDS
30 × 22 in., 76 × 56 cm.
Private collection

1973
PAINTINGS,
OIL ON CANVAS

1. SOLITAIRE
71 × 79 in., 180 × 200 cm.
Fischer Fine Arts Ltd., London
Knoedler Gallery, Inc., New York

2. CIRCUS, CIRCUS
80 × 70 in., 203 × 178 cm.
Coll. Denise Lindner, New York

3. L'AS DE TRÈFLE
79 × 71 in., 200 × 180 cm.
Private collection

WATERCOLORS

1. TÊTE D'HOMME
27 × 19 in., 68 × 49 cm.
Musée National d'Art Moderne, Paris
Fonds National d'Art Contemporain

2. GIRL WITH BIRD
12 × 9 in., 31 × 24 cm.
Private collection

3. UNTITLED
17 × 13 in., 43 × 33 cm.
Coll. Henri Cartier-Bresson, Paris

Biographical Chronology
1968 to 1974
Bibliography

BIOGRAPHICAL CHRONOLOGY

1901
Born in Hamburg of American mother.
Moves with his parents to Nuremberg.

1922-1924
Studies at the Kunstgewerbeschule.

1924-1927
Moves to Munich and attends first the Kunstgewerbeschule, then the Akademie der Bildenden Künste.

1927-1928
Spends two years in Berlin.

1929-1933
Returns to Munich and becomes the art director of the Knorr and Hirth publishing house.

1933
Escapes to Paris after the Nazis' rise to power. Joins other refugees in political activities, continues to paint, meets with French artists, works occasionally as a graphic artist.

1939
Interned by the French government for political reasons at the start of the Second World War, released five months later. Joins the French and later the British armies.

1941
Emigrates to the United States and settles in New York. Works as an illustrator of books and magazines such as *Vogue, Fortune* and *Harper's Bazaar*, meets with the artists of the New York School as well as with refugee artists from Europe.

1948
Becomes an American citizen.

1950
Starts painting full time.

1952-1965
Teaches at the Pratt Institute, originates a course called "Creative Expression."

1957
Receives the William and Norma Copley Foundation Award.
Lectures at the Yale University School of Art and Architecture.

1965
Guest lecturer at the Hochschule für Bildende Kunst, Hamburg

1968
Marries Denise. Lives in Paris and New York.

ONE MAN EXHIBITIONS

Betty Parsons Gallery, New York, 1954
Betty Parsons Gallery, New York, 1956
Betty Parsons Gallery, New York, 1959
Daniel Cordier and Michel Warren, New York, 1961
Robert Fraser Gallery, London, 1963
Cordier and Ekstrom Gallery, New York, 1963
Cordier and Ekstrom Gallery, New York, 1964
Galerie Claude Bernard, Paris, 1965
Galerie Galatea, Turin, 1965
Cordier and Ekstrom Gallery, New York, 1965
U.S.A. Travelling show organized by the Museum of Modern Art, New York, 1966-68 (Graphics)
Cordier and Ekstrom Gallery, New York, 1967
Städtisches Museum Schloss Morsbroich, Leverkusen, 1968
Kestner Gesellschaft, Hanover, 1968
Staatliche Kunsthalle, Baden-Baden, 1969
Haus am Waldsee, West Berlin, 1969
University Art Museum, University of California, Berkeley, 1969
Walker Art Center, Minneapolis, Minnesota, 1969
Galerie Boisserée, Cologne, 1971
Spencer A. Samuels Gallery, New York, 1971 (Watercolors)

MONOGRAPHS

ASHTON, DORE. *Richard Lindner*. 1969. New York.

DIENST, ROLF-GUNTER. *Richard Lindner*. 1969. New York.

GENERAL WORKS

ALLEY, RONALD. *Recent American Art*. 1969. London, p. 9, pl. 22.

DELEUZE, GILLES. GUATTARI, FELIX. *Capitalisme et schizophrénie. L'Anti-Œdipe*. 1972. Paris, pp. 13, 55, 429.

DIENST, ROLF-GUNTER. *Positionen*. 1968. Köln, pp. 69-72.

— *Graphic USA*. 1968. Baden-Baden.

HUNTER, SAM. *American Art of the Twentieth Century*. 1972. New York.

KAHMEN, VOLKER. *Erotic Art Today*. 1971. Greenwich, Connecticut.

LANGUI, EMILE. "L'expressionnisme depuis 1945 et le mouvement Cobra" in *Depuis 45. L'art de notre temps*. 1970. Bruxelles, Vol. II, pp. 74, 90, 95, 152, pl. 84.

LIPPARD, LUCY R. *Pop Art*. 1966. London, pp. 118, 133.

RUSSELL, JOHN. GABLIK, SUZI. *Pop Art Redefined*. 1969. London.

ARTICLES

ADRIAN, DENNIS. "New York." *Art Forum*, Vol. 5, No 7, III/1967, pp. 55-58.

ALBRIGHT, THOMAS. "Pop People in a Plastic World." *This World, San Francisco Chronicle*, VI/22, 1969, pp. 30-31.

ALEXANDRE, ALEXANDRE. "Das Plakat als Kunstwerk: ein Beitrag zum Schaffen Richard Lindners." *Das Kunstwerk*, Vol. II, No 5-6, 1948, pp. 27-31.

AMBERG, G. "Richard Lindner." *Graphis*, Vol. 5, No 25, 1949, pp. 8-13.

ASHTON, DORE. "Show at the Cordier and Warren Gallery." *Arts and Architecture*, Vol. 79, II/1962, p. 6.

— "Art USA 1962." *Studio*, No 163, III/1962, p. 91.

— "Americans 1963 at The Museum of Modern Art." *Arts and Architecture*, No 80, VII/1963, p. 4.

— "Richard Lindner, the secret of the inner voice." *Studio International*, No 849, I/1964, pp. 12-17.

— "New York Gallery Notes." *Art in America*, Vol. 55, No 1, I/II/1967, p. 91.

— "It's a Big Country." *Studio*, Vol. 173, No 887, III/1967, pp. 153-154.

— "An open and shut case. Allusions to specific sensuous experiences of space." *Arts Magazine*, IV/1968, p. 28.

— "Richard Lindner's Eternal Return." *Arts Magazine*, V/1969, pp. 48-50.

BARO, G. "Gathering of Americans." *Arts*, Vol. 37, IX/1963, p. 33.

BENEDIKT, MICHAEL. "New York, Eroticism of Late." *Art International*, Vol. II, No 4, IV/20, 1967, p. 65.

BORSICK, HELEN. "His Art: Neither Pop Nor Op but Lindner." *Cleveland Plain Dealer*, IV/14, 1966.

CANADAY, JOHN. "Lindner's Apocalyptic Honkytonk." *The New York Times*, IV/27, 1969.

CORDIER, ROBERT. "Richard Lindner." *Zoom*, No 20, IX/X/1973, pp. 66-79.

CRONE, RAINER. "Uptown, bei Lindner. Ein Gespräch mit dem deutschamerikanischen Maler." *Die Welt*, IV/10, 1970.

DIENST, ROLF-GUNTER. "Richard Lindner." *Das Kunstwerk*, Vol. 19, VIII/1965, p. 21.

— "Lindner." *Das Kunstwerk*, Vol. 20, II/III/1967, pp. 5-6.

— "Die Documenta IV." *Das Kunstwerk*, Vol. 21, VIII/1968, p. 36.

FRANK, SUZANNE. "Richard Lindner remakes the New York scene." *Arts Magazine*, XII/I/1970, pp. 32-33.

FRIGERIO, SIMONE. "Les expositions à Paris." *Aujourd'hui*, No 50, VII/1965, pp. 86-87.

GASSER, MANUEL. "Richard Lindner's Fun City." *Graphis*, No 152, 1970-71, pp. 496-503.

GRAY, CAMILLA. "Drawings for Art in America's 50th Anniversary." *Art in America*, Vol. 51, II/1963, p. 65.

HAHN, OTTO. "Lettre de Paris." *Art International*, Vol. 9, No 6, IX/1965, p. 72.

HENNING, E.B. "German Expressionist Paintings" (Cleveland Museum of Art). *Burlington Magazine*, Vol. 108, XII/1966, pp. 632-633.

HESS, THOMAS B. "Phony Crisis in American Art." *Art News*, Vol. 62, 1963, p. 28.

KELLY, E.T. "Neo-Dada: a critique of Pop Art." *Art Journal*, Vol. 23, No 3, 1964, p. 200.

KRAMER, HILTON. "Lindner's Ladies." *Playboy*, III/1973, pp. 96-101.

KUDIELKA, ROBERT. "Germany: The New Objectivity." *Studio International*, III/1969, pp. 84-89.

LEVEQUE, JEAN-JACQUES. "Richard Lindner." *La Nouvelle Revue Française*, Vol. XII, No 154, X/1965, pp. 735-736.

LIPPARD, LUCY. "New York Letter." *Art International*, Vol. 9, No 3, IV/1965, pp. 55-56.

LYOTARD, JEAN-FRANÇOIS. "Les filles machines folles de Lindner." *Art Vivant*, No 41, VII/1973, pp. 8-9.

MELVILLE, ROBERT. "First London Exhibition." *Architectural Review*, Vol. 132, XI/1962, p. 363.

— "Obsessive Image." *Architectural Review*, Vol. 143, VI/1968, p. 465.

O'DOHERTY, BRIAN. "Lindner's Private but Very Modern Hades." *New York Times*, III/8/1964.

P.B. "Marilyn Monroe repose en pièces." *L'Express*, No 862, XII/25/1967.

PEASE, ROLAND F. "Avant-garde artists band together to assist dance, music, theatre." *Art voices*, II/1963.

PENROSE, ROLAND. "Richard Lindner." *Art International*, Vol. 11, I/1967, pp. 30-33.

PERREAULT, JOHN. "Venus in Vinyl." *Art News*, Vol. 65, I/1967, pp. 46-48.

PICARD, LIL. "The Turn of the Brush." *East Village Center*, I/15, 1967, p. 14.

R.D. *Art News*, VII/1969, pp. 17-18.

REICHARDT, JASIA. "Les expositions à l'étranger: Londres." *Aujourd'hui*, Vol. 6, IX/1962, p. 58.

ROBERTS, C. "Lettre de New York." *Aujourd'hui*, Vol. 6, II/1962, pp. 26-29.

— "Les expositions à New York." *Aujourd'hui*, Vol. 8, II/1962, pp. 26-29.

ROBBINS, DANIEL. "The Albert Pilavin Collection: Twentieth Century American Art." *Bulletin of Rhode Island School of Design Museum Notes*, Vol. 55, No 4, V/1969, pp. 34-37.

ROSENBLUM, ROBERT. "Sophisticated Primitive: Exhibition at Parsons Gallery." *Art Digest*, II/15/1954, p. 13.

ROSENTHAL, N. "Six-Day Bicycle Wheel Race: Multiple Originals." *Art in America*, Vol. 53, X/1965, p. 101.

ROTZLER, WILLY. "Richard Lindners Panoptikum." *Du*, IX/1970, pp. 669-670.

SANDLER, IRVING H. "New York Letter." *Art International*, Vol. 5, No 9, XI/20, 1961, p. 56.

SCHMIED, WIELAND. "Richard Lindner." *Merian* (Hamburg), Vol. 23, No 9, p. 73.

— "Richard Lindner and the human being as a toy." *Studio International*, No 906, XII/1968, pp. 252-5.

SCHRODER, THOMAS. "Hunger nach Kunst? Guten Appetit!" *Tween Magazine*, XI/1970.

SCHWARTZ, NANCY. "Oskar Schlemmer, An Interview with Richard Lindner." *Arts Magazine*, XI/1969.

SECKLER, D.G. "Artist in America: Victim of the Culture Boom?" *Art in America*, Vol. 51, XII/1963, p. 35.

SPIES, WERNER. "Peep-shows, Body Painting und Hair." *Frankfurter Allgemeine Zeitung*, VI/21, 1969.

— "Das exportierte Europa — Richard Lindner der Maler New Yorks wird siebzig." *Frankfurter Allgemeine Zeitung*, XI/11, 1971.

— "Die Maschinerie des Unbehagens. Richard Lindners Suche nach Marcel Proust/zu zwei Porträts des Malers." *Frankfurter Allgemeine Zeitung*, I/3, 1973, p. 24.

— "Wappentiere der Gesellschaft." *Frankfurter Allgemeine Zeitung.*

STEVENSON, WADE. "Les secrets de Richard Lindner." *XXe Siècle*, Vol. 40, VI/1973, pp. 144-147.

SWANSON, DEAN. "Richard Lindner, a painter of figures, unique, brilliantly erotic." *Vogue*, No 15, VIII/1969.

TILLIM, SIDNEY. "John Graham and Richard Lindner." *Arts*, Vol. 36, XI/1961, pp. 34-37.

— "Richard Lindner." *Aujourd'hui*, Vol. 6, II/1962, pp. 26-29.

WHITTET, G.S. "First London Exhibition." *Studio*, Vol. 164, IX/1962, p. 116.

WILLARD, C. "Drawings Today." *Art in America*, Vol. 52, X/1964, p. 64.

"Tales of Hoffmann, Review." *Magazine of Art*, Vol. 40, V/1947, p. 204.

"First One-Man Show in America at Parsons Gallery." *Art News*, Vol. 52, II/1954, p. 44.

"Exhibition of Paintings and Drawings at Parsons Gallery." *Arts*, Vol. 30, III/1956, p. 57.

"Exhibition at Parsons." *Art News*, No 57, II/1959, p. 15.

"Exhibition at Cordier and Warren Gallery." *Art News*, No 60, X/1961, pp. 10-11.

"Americans 1963 at Museum of Modern Art, New York." *Art International*, Vol. 7, No 6, VI/1963, p. 77.

"Richard Lindner — One-Man Show." *New York Times*, III/8, 1964.

"Stop, Caution, Go." *Newsweek*, III/9, 1964.

"Painter of the Grass Crowd; Show at Manhattan's Cordier and Ekstrom Gallery." *Time*, III/20, 1964, p. 70.

"Exhibition at Cordier and Ekstrom Gallery." *Art News*, No 63, III/1964, p. 10.

"Collages and Paintings at Cordier and Ekstrom." *Art News*, No 64, IV/1965, p. 11.

"Richard Lindner — One-Man Show." *New York Times*, I/22, 1966.

"Baal Booster." *Time*, II/3, 1967, p. 44.

"Exhibition at Cordier and Ekstrom Gallery." *Art Forum*, Vol. 15, III/1967, pp. 55-56.

"Richard Lindner: the Rubens of the love generation." *Avant Garde*, I/1968.

"Lindner, Mutters Rätsel." *Der Spiegel*, No 44, X/28, 1968.

"Rummel mit Robotern." *Der Spiegel*, III/3, 1969, pp. 138-139.

"Warum Richard Lindner Maschinenfrauen malt." *Tween*, Vol. 6, VI/1969.

"Richard Lindner." *Art International*, Vol. XIII, No 6, 1969, p. 49.

"Richard Lindner." *Art Now* (New York), Vol. 2, No 11, 1971.

EXHIBITION CATALOGUES

Paris, Galerie Claude Bernard, 1965.

Roma, Galleria Il fante di Spade, and Torino, Galleria Galatea, 1965 (text: Luigi Carluccio).

Leverkusen, Städtisches Museum, Schloss Morsbroich, and Baden-Baden, Staatliche Kunsthalle, 1969 (texts: Wieland Schmied, Rolf-Gunter Dienst, Sidney Tillim, Roland Penrose).

Hannover, Kestner Gesellschaft, 1968-69 (texts: Wieland Schmied, Rolf Wedewer, Rolf-Gunter Dienst).

Berkeley, University Art Museum, University of California, and Minneapolis, Walker Art Center, 1969 (text: Dore Ashton; interview: Dean Swanson).

New York, Spencer A. Samuels and Company, Ltd., 1971 (*Fun City*, original watercolours).

Paris, Musée National d'Art Moderne; Rotterdam, Musée Boymans van Beuningen; Düsseldorf, Kunsthalle, and Zurich, Kunsthaus, 1974 (texts: Jean-Hubert Martin; interview: Wolfgang G. Fischer).

Assistant Editor: Béatrice Conrad-Eybesfeld
Design: Jacques Combet
Research: Silvelin Costinescu, Jane Salzfass
Photography: Guy Bazzuri, Walter Drayer, Harry Hess, Jacqueline Hyde, Paul Katz, Robert E. Mates, Musées Nationaux-France, Pascal Perkis, Eric Pollitzer, Shorewood Photography, Rodney Todd-White
Halftones: I.R.L., Novacoop
Color Separations: Alfried Holle, I.R.L., Loga Chrome, Novacoop, S.I.P.R.
First printing completed February 15th, 1975 at Imprimeries Réunies S.A., Lausanne, Switzerland

DATE DUE